Careers as a Flight Attendant: Flight to the Future

By
Catherine Okray Lobus

The Rosen Publishing Group, Inc.
New York

Published in 1991, 1996 by The Rosen Publishing Group, Inc.
29 East 21st Street, New York, New York 10010

Revised Edition 1996

Manufactured in the United States of America.

Library of Congress Cataloging-in-Publication Data

Lobus, Catherine Okray.
Careers as a flight attendant: flight to the future/by Catherine Okray Lobus.—rev. ed.
p. cm.
Includes bibliographical references and index.
Summary: Readers explore the possible challenges, rewards, drawbacks, and "glamour" of a career as a flight attendant.
ISBN 0-8239-1953-6
1. Flight attendants—Vocational guidance—Juvenile literature. [1. Flight attendants—Vocational guidance. 2. Vocational guidance.] I. Title.
HD8039.A43L63 1996
387.7'42—dc20 90-21437
CIP
AC

It is said that an angel must earn its wings. This is sometimes accomplished by the completion of an assigned task, usually helping some hapless mortal, and generally with very little cooperation from said beneficiary. Tradition has it that when the angel is successful it receives its wings, and at that moment a bell rings somewhere on the earth.

This book is dedicated with love to Vicy Morris Young, for when I got my wings, a small silver bell rang in this world; not for me, but for her. She gave me the best there is—somewhere to belong.

About the Author

Catherine Okray Lobus is a native of Southern California. She was recruited by both Eastern and United Airlines while attending Cerritos Junior College. "I chose United because I thought their uniforms were better looking. It simply never occurred to me that had I chosen Eastern I could have trained in Miami in December instead of Chicago. I doubt I would have chosen differently, but since then I have tried to make my decisions based on fact instead of fancy."

After two and a half years, Ms. Lobus left United to marry. Aviation opportunities being somewhat limited at the time in her new home town of Las Vegas, she spent the next eight years in food and beverage management for private clubs and casino dining rooms. In the deregulation boom of the 1980s, she returned to flying and held various management positions from Supervisor to Director with several charter and scheduled carriers in the area.

Ms. Lobus is now an owner and partner in Airline Resources, Inc., a full-service aviation consulting firm that specializes in airline certification, manual and training program development, organizational restructuring, route and feasibility studies, financial audit, business plans, and management contracts.

Acknowledgments

I wish to thank all those tireless, wonderful, and cooperative people without whose assistance and moral support this book would not exist.

My business partner, Marino Johannsson, for technical advice and infinite patience; Mom and Dad for moral support and proofreading; all those who gave of their time and effort in order to answer and return the surveys; Wayne Brinkman of Simmons Airlines; Terri Morgan, Casino Express; Maureen Van Bruggen, Henson; Michael Bjorklund, Midway; Dave Carroll, Southwest; Kathleen Duffy, American Airlines; Mr. Boyle from United, and the folks at Alaska and Skywest.

Thanks also to Diane Abbott for the telephone support; to all the wonderful people I worked with over the years who helped make every day a memory, especially Frank Fleischmann, Jack Holland, Capt. Bill O'Hara, Capt Boyd Michael, and my best friend as well as the best "Lady Pilot"—oh, heck, maybe the best pilot in the whole world, Bea Ramu-Hoskins, who have all in their own way contributed to the history, wonder, and fun of aviation; to my buddy Tami H. for the menu help; to my favorite Federal Inspectors, Gary and Lou, who thought this book was timely; and to Suzie Wilkins-Roberts, Kathy Santos-Mann, and Bonnie Krismann-Cronin—older is better.

Contents

Introduction

Ladies and Gentlemen:

On behalf of Imaginary Airlines, I'd like to welcome you aboard a charter flight to the future. All passengers aboard the airplane share the desire to learn all that they can about flight attendant careers.

Our special flight will begin, as all flights do, by examining the preparations that you must make now to ensure a safe and comfortable journey. After these preparations, we will identify the steps involved in selecting the type of carrier for which you would like to work. We will look at the application process and the interview phase of your job search. In addition, we will discuss what to expect from the training process.

Throughout our journey, we will focus on the realities of life as a flight attendant. We will discuss the "glamour myth," look at the possibilities of promotion, consider long-term job stability, and identify the types of rewards and drawbacks that may be expected.

Please fasten your seatbelts. We will be taking off soon. Thank you for choosing Imaginary Airlines. We wish you a pleasant flight.

1

Check-in: Personal Profile Checklist

Flight attendant careers appeal to many people because of the travel involved. Not only do you travel on the job, but you also receive travel discounts to use on your days off. The possibility of seeing the world is exciting, and flight attendant careers often are considered glamorous.

Working as a flight attendant, however, also can be demanding. It is a people-oriented career, and sometimes working with people can be stressful. Not all passengers are pleasant and quiet. In fact, some can be rude and loud. Passengers who board a flight have stresses in their own lives, and these stresses often affect passengers' behavior toward members of the flight crew.

Airlines try very hard to identify people who possess the qualities that will lead to successful flight attendant careers. But because of the incredible number of people interviewed and hired each year, occasionally someone with a personality not quite suited for flight attendant work slips through the hiring process.

Have you ever traveled on an airplane where one of the flight attendants seemed angry and miserable, or not at all happy with his or her job? This attitude probably made you feel uncomfortable and unwelcome, and you may have thought to yourself that next time you would travel on a different airline.

Each passenger on this Imaginary Airlines flight should begin his or her journey by identifying the personality traits he or she possesses. Flight attendants are considered ambassadors for their airline; they may be seen by hundreds of members of the public each day. Because of their high profile, flight attendants at some airlines are considered part of the company's marketing department. In fact, more carriers are beginning to refer to flight attendants as CSRs, or Customer Service Representatives.

Certain key personality traits should be possessed by anyone considering a flight attendant career. Having these qualities will improve your ability to be a success in this career.

Read through the checklist of desired personality traits below. Look at each item and be truthful to yourself about whether or not you possess this quality.

Personality Traits	*Yes*	*No*	*Sometimes*
1. I truly like people.			
2. I am flexible.			
3. I am self-disciplined.			
4. I am a self-starter.			
5. I would rather be a leader than a follower.			
6. I always follow through on a project.			
7. I am a happy person.			
8. I always follow the rules.			
9. I have lots of energy.			
10. I have respect for authority.			
11. I perform well under stress.			
12. I am healthy.			
13. I take pride in myself and in my appearance.			
14. I have good communication skills.			
15. I work well on a team.			

If you answered "Yes" to all of the above qualities, you are likely to be a person who will be successful in a flight attendant career. An occasional "Sometimes" answer can be acceptable, depending on the question, but any "No" answer is a warning that being a flight attendant may not be an appropriate career for you.

DESIRED PERSONALITY TRAITS

1. **I truly like people.**

Flight attendants work with all types of people in a very close environment. If you've ever been on an airplane that is filled to capacity, you are familiar with the small area in which flight attendants must work. On an international flight, for example, a flight attendant could spend 12 or more hours in an enclosed environment with the same 400 people, and there may be only 14 flight attendants to work with them.

During that time, some passengers will become ill, and some will become fearful. Most of them will be hungry, thirsty, tired, and even cranky. Babies will cry, the restroom lines will get long, and everyone will begin to wonder if the flight will ever end.

If you do not enjoy working with people, you certainly will be unhappy working on a flight like this. You may even consider a career change. Yet at the end of a flight—even a difficult one—a flight attendant is expected to be smiling and thanking everyone for choosing that particular airline. These friendly actions are good customer service and often influence people to fly the same carrier again.

2. **I am flexible.**

Many people are attracted to flight attendant careers because of the element of change involved in the job. A flight attendant's schedule usually changes from one day to the next. You may work nights or weekends, early mornings or late afternoons.

Airlines operate 24 hours a day, 365 days a year—including holidays. If you are a day person and cannot adjust to working all night, you may want to reconsider the flight attendant career. If you must have Sundays off, or if you can't imagine spending Christmas Eve in a hotel in Cleveland, look into other work.

All airlines work on a seniority system. When you graduate from training, you are a junior. That means that you are assigned to the flights that are left after everyone else has chosen the flights that they want.

3. **I am self-disciplined.**

One big attraction of the flight attendant profession is the idea that the job requires little supervision. All crew members are expected to know their jobs and to perform tasks as a team. You are expected to arrive on time and to work long hours if needed.

This can be difficult if you have worked some long flights, arrived home very late, had little time to sleep, and are expected to be back on the job early the next morning. There are times when you'll want nothing more than to roll over and go back to sleep. But consider the consequences of doing just that: You make your crew late, which makes the airplane late, which makes the passengers late. Because *you* did not get out of bed, some people have missed their flight connections or their business meetings. All of this can have a negative monetary and customer-relations impact on your company.

The airline industry, which schedules its flights by taking into consideration cost effectiveness and weather, traffic, and mechanical delays, can provide situations of minimum rest and maximum working hours for its employees. It's only natural for your body to rebel against the stresses it is asked to endure. Before embarking on a flight attendant career, you must ask yourself whether or not you will be able to conquer your body's natural desire to be comfortable in order to fulfill your commitment to your company.

4. **I am a self-starter.**

This personality requirement again relates to flight attendants' lack of direct supervision. Flight attendants receive their position assignments at a preflight briefing. When you receive your assignment, you must be familiar with the duties required for that assignment, and you must perform them efficiently and immediately. Failure to do your job properly could have embarrassing results.

For example, if you are responsible for the galley supplies but waited too long to count the meals, or failed to report any shortage to the senior flight attendant, you could be responsible for several passengers going hungry. This most likely would upset those passengers, leading to a negative company image and embarrassing the other flight attendants.

When you work as a flight attendant, you are not reminded to do your job. No one will check to make sure you are performing the required tasks; your fellow crew members will assume that you are doing your part of the work. Even "sometimes" self-starters have no place in a flight attendant career.

5. **I would rather be a leader than a follower.**

The different tasks performed by flight attendants require varying degrees of leadership ability. Although you can be a successful flight attendant if you "sometimes" possess this personality trait, you should continue to improve your leadership abilities.

Passengers usually expect you, as the flight attendant,

to lead them through the requirements of the flight. This can mean giving general information to a first-time flier or directing confused passengers in case of an emergency. You are considered the authority in what is a generally unfamiliar environment.

Additional leadership skills are required after you gain experience as a flight attendant. Those beginning work for an airline are directed by the senior flight attendant. The requirements needed to achieve the senior position vary from airline to airline. Some airlines have a time requirement; for example, after three to six months as a junior, you would be qualified to be a senior. With other airlines you must bid to upgrade your level or perhaps complete more schooling or pass a test. At the same time, senior flight attendants earn higher salaries as compensation for their increased responsibility.

6. **I always follow through on a project.**

In flight attendant training you are taught that "No one is finished until everyone is finished." The goal of a flight attendant is to make all passengers as comfortable as possible during a flight and then to put everything away so it looks as if nothing had been disturbed. The reasons behind this are safety-related. For instance, items in the aircraft cabin must be secured during landing. If this is not done properly, passengers could be injured by carry-on items that move around. To prepare an aircraft for landing, the entire flight crew must work together, and each member must complete his or her individual tasks.

After the plane lands and you have thanked the last passenger on the last flight of the day, your airplane should look as it did when you boarded it six cities ago. When this is done, you pick up all of the items that you brought on board and go home.

7. **I am a happy person.**

This personality trait is not required at all times. It is unrealistic to expect a person to be happy every minute in a day. However, it is realistic to expect flight attendants to be basically good-natured people who seldom complain.

Airline passengers have certain expectations of flight attendants. They expect to be assisted by a flight attendant who is happy, confident, and eager to please. They do not want to hear about the flight crew's personal problems, the injustices of a new union contract, or your opinion of the latest aviation-related legislation on Capitol Hill.

The satisfaction of having and doing a job that you love should be a great incentive to happiness. But for that to happen, you should be naturally inclined to feel happy. If you take a dark view of the world and have difficulty identifying reasons to feel happy, most likely you should consider another area of work.

8. **I always follow the rules.**

A "Yes" is the only acceptable answer to this personality trait.

The airline industry is highly regulated. You must learn, enforce, and abide by rules set by your company, by the Federal Aviation Administration (FAA), and by the Department of Transportation (DOT). In fact, the FAA and DOT rules are not only rules; they are laws. The consequences of violating the laws set by these governing agencies can include being prosecuted as a criminal, paying a fine, and going to jail.

FAA and DOT regulations are discussed in Chapter 4.

9. **I have lots of energy.**

You may be a couch potato at home, but you will certainly get your share of exercise walking on the flight between Los Angeles and London. During that flight you will serve cocktails, second cocktails, dinner with wine, coffee, liqueurs, and hot towels. Then you will pass out pillows and blankets and turn on the movie. (No, you don't get to watch the movie.)

You then set up a bar so that anyone who doesn't want to sleep will have easy access to anything they want or need. After a while you collect the pillows and blankets, pass out toothbrushes, and serve breakfast with champagne, coffee, and juice.

After you clean all that up, you sell duty-free merchandise. Finally, you prepare for landing. Once the plane has arrived, you help passengers find their carry-on items, and you wish them a pleasant day.

If you don't have enough energy left over to change your clothes and jump on the tube—the subway—for a quick visit to downtown London, you're going to miss one of the best parts of being a flight attendant.

In training, I tell my new flight attendants that they can sleep when they get old (whenever that is). With one or two notable exceptions, every place in the world has something new and different to offer, no matter how often you have been there. Whenever I flew a trip, I chose to become the social director for the crew and took responsibility for organizing the day's activities. I have arranged everything from a tour of the Tower of London to an excursion to the Shamrock Bar and Grill in Lamella, Nevada. We always had fun, and that showed in our attitude toward our passengers and our ability to function as a crew.

If you only "sometimes" have energy, you can get by as long as you reserve it for your work time. Be aware, however, that you may be cheating yourself out of something irreplaceable: a chance to grow as a person under circumstances not afforded to most people, and a chance to forge friendships with your coworkers that can last a lifetime.

10. **I have respect for authority.**

The captain is the ultimate authority on an airline flight. If you should happen to dislike him or her, you must be able to set aside your feelings and follow the orders given. Passengers' lives can depend on your ability to follow the directions given by the airplane captain.

There is no compromise answer to this question.

11. **I perform well under stress.**

Those considering careers as flight attendants must perform well in stressful situations. From the initial interview with an airline to the actual day-to-day tasks of the job, flight attendants are faced with varying levels of stress throughout their careers.

One of the first things an airline interviewer looks for is a candidate who is poised and self-assured. An interview can be a stressful situation. It is normal to be a little nervous; after all, this is what you want more than anything, and you want to make a good first impression. However, if you are too nervous to answer a simple question, or if your body language shouts agitation rather than animation, you probably will not be hearing from that airline again.

Flight attendant training is extremely intense. You can be tested on what you learn as often as every day, with a required grade of up of 90 percent. One failure may be enough to dismiss you from the program.

Airlines have weight requirements for members of the flight crew. During training, you may be weighed every day or once a week. Too much pizza can result in a one-way ticket home.

Throughout training, you will be observed by *everyone*

regarding your manner of dress, your conduct, and your attitude. This living under constant, critical observation can prove very stressful.

After you graduate, you face another set of stresses. Line flying requires that you always be on time and always look your best. You must be gracious and competent and professional, no matter what the conditions are. You must be able to handle any illness or emergency, large or small, without falling apart.

"Yes," you must possess this very important personality trait to have a successful career as a flight attendant.

12. **I am healthy.**

To be a successful flight attendant, you need a basically fit and healthy body. You need to be able to withstand the physical conditions of high-altitude flying and the irregularities of the lifestyle.

Besides high-altitude stresses on your body, you may experience jet lag or be required to work during bad weather. Also, you are in a sealed environment with many chances for exposure to the more mundane types of illness, such as colds and flu.

Some illnesses are less likely, but there is a minimal chance of contracting them. For example, depending on the route your carrier flies, you may come in contact with circumstances for contracting such diseases as dysentery, yellow fever, or malaria.

Even healthy people catch colds and fall ill. You will not be expected to be in top health every day of your career. But in general, you need a strong and healthy constitution to be a flight attendant.

13. **I take pride in my appearance.**

Flight attendants represent the airline for which they work. Passengers will notice if your clothing is wrinkled or your hair is a mess. They may wonder if the entire airline is run in a sloppy manner. For this reason, the cleanliness and general appearance of a flight attendant is important. Be aware that your personal attitude toward yourself is of great importance in gaining and keeping a position as a flight attendant.

14. **I have good communication skills.**

Flight attendants must be able to communicate effectively with the passengers of the airline. Passengers rely on the flight crew to relay information about the rules and regulations of the airline, as well as about emergency procedures. Even information about the meal of the day, the in-flight movie, and connecting flights must be communicated by flight attendants.

Flight attendants often face further challenges when communicating with passengers from other countries or with those who are deaf or hearing-impaired. They must be open and willing to try to communicate with all passengers aboard a flight.

If speaking in front of a group or communicating with someone who speaks little English makes you nervous or uncomfortable, perhaps you should consider another career.

15. **I work well on a team.**

A flight attendant is one member of an entire flight crew. The crew includes fellow flight attendants, the senior flight attendant, the captain and cocaptain, and other members in the cockpit. All these people must be willing to work together as a team.

One aspect of working successfully on a team is completing the tasks expected of him or her. A team member who does not do what is expected could be placing the entire flight in danger.

Good team members also must be willing to work

with people they don't particularly like. If you dislike one of the other team members and try not to work with that person, your job may be adversely affected.

For example, animosity toward the senior flight attendant may affect both your personality and your actions. You may be discourteous to a passenger or fail to be helpful. Such an attitude can make passengers angry at both you and the airline. In addition, you could place passengers in danger by choosing to ignore the senior's orders.

On each flight you are a member of a flight team. The team members will constantly change. Some you will like; others you may loathe. No matter what the case, you must make every effort to work with them—for the efficiency of the flight and for the safety of the passengers.

Rewards of a Flight Attendant Career

The items on the checklist might be considered by some to be drawbacks to a career as a flight attendant. They are meant to give you a realistic portrayal of the field. Every profession has rewards to balance any drawbacks. If you have chosen a career suitable to you, the positive aspects always outweigh the negative.

The most obvious reward of working for an airline is free and reduced-rate travel benefits for yourself and your spouse, children, and parents. Most hotels, car rental agencies, and cruise lines offer reduced room rates. You can travel almost anywhere in the world almost as cheaply as other people vacation in a neighboring city.

You also have the time to enjoy it. The more senior you become, the fewer days you have to work per month. Some senior people work only ten out of thirty days. Being new is not bad, however. Most airlines have liberal trip-trade policies so that you can arrange a heavy work schedule in one part of the month and have the rest of the month off.

When working, instead of going home at the end of the day, you sometimes have what is called a layover or RON (Remain Over Night). You could end up in any city in the world for from twelve hours to several days—all at the expense of your company.

Most companies have excellent benefits in the areas of insurance, retirement plans, credit unions, stock purchase, and dry-cleaning reimbursement. Such things may not seem very important to you now, but they will in the future.

Then there are the more personal rewards.

You have tremendous independence. We have discussed the absence of direct supervision in your work, which affords you a freedom not found in other career fields. Each day is different, bringing with it new experiences and challenges. You also have a say in what type of schedule you work.

If you so choose, you will be able to form very close friendships with people who share your values and interests. You will have the opportunity to grow and prosper as a person by virtue of the variety of people with whom you are in daily contact.

Your training will instill in you a sense of responsibility and a degree of self-confidence that some people are never able to achieve, no matter how much time and money they spend on books and seminars. This confidence is so evident that strangers will stop you in airports and even on the street to ask for directions or advice. You may not think this odd, but it is when you are not wearing your uniform!

Finally, there is the ultimate reward of knowing that you can make some small difference in someone's life. You can calm a fear, ease a pain, or turn a bad day into a good one. If you truly like people, the deep satisfaction you feel in helping and pleasing them cannot be measured by any standard.

There you have it, the good and the bad. If you still feel that a career as a flight attendant is for you, let's go on to the next step on our Imaginary Airlines Flight to the Future, the Preflight Check, and see what you should be doing now to enhance your chances of attaining this goal.

2

The Preflight Check: Minimum Qualifications

Flight attendants begin their working days by performing specific duties aboard an airplane in preparation for the flight. Each attendant is assigned a particular area of the plane to check. One may verify that all the emergency equipment is in place, secure, and functioning. Another may check galley supplies, and yet another might check customer-service or "comfort" kits, which include such things as bandages, aspirin, disposable diapers, and motion sickness medicine. (The contents vary depending on the airline.) This entire process is called the *preflight check*.

Throughout the preflight check, flight attendants work to make sure that everything they might need during a flight is ready and available. You, too, as passengers on this Imaginary Airlines flight, can perform a preflight check. But your duties will include identifying the minimum qualifications involved in becoming a flight attendant and analyzing your skills to decide if a flight attendant career is right for you.

Former Qualifications

Several qualifications that were once applicable are no longer used to weed out potential flight attendants. For nearly twenty years, gender has not been a barrier. As a matter of fact, the very first flight attendants in the 1920s were men. They were called *stewards*. The first female flight attendants were not hired until 1930. Through the years, men continued to work in inflight service, but they were hired usually for specific positions such as International Purser and Hawaiian Steward. Although most domestic flying as we know it today was reserved for female flight attendants, men certainly made their contribution to the profession.

In the early 1970s, as the result of a court decision, it became unlawful to discriminate against anyone applying for an inflight position on the basis of gender. The title "stewardess" was dropped because of the growing numbers of men who applied for and won positions in the cabin, and the job classification of "flight attendant" became the legal and accepted terminology.

Personal status qualifications also no longer applied. Until the late 1960s, no female flight attendant could be married and retain her position. In the early 1970s, you could not be hired if married, but you could marry once flying and not be grounded. Today, whether male or female, your personal life is no one's business except your own. You can be hired if you are married, even if you have children.

You should consider, however, that an airline is not going to accommodate itself to your needs. Your personal life is your own problem. If you are married and you are hired by a carrier that wants to base you in London, that will put a strain on your relationship if your spouse is in Omaha. Your spouse or children may not want to leave their home to be with you in Chicago, for example, and so you may be away from them on your wedding anniversary or your child's birthday.

This does not mean that you cannot have a successful personal relationship while working as a flight attendant.

Most flight attendants do. It is important to research the airlines at which you apply for a job. Check the airlines that have bases in the city or part of the country in which you live. Or consider a commuter airline that will have you home every night. They do exist.

CURRENT QUALIFICATIONS

Airlines do have specific requirements regarding the height, weight, vision, health, education, and age of their employees. Carriers also have preferences regarding work experience.

Height

Item number one on our preflight checklist is height. In general, you must be a minimum of 5′2″ and a maximum of 6′2″. Do not despair, however, if you are a little "short" of this requirement. Some commuter airplane and helicopter operators seek candidates of smaller stature because of low ceilings in their aircraft. Other airlines hire flight attendants taller than 6′2″ because they operate larger planes with very high ceiling panels.

Be sure to research the height requirements of the companies for which you are interested in working. Height specifications were established for a purpose: You must be tall enough to reach equipment on the plane, even if it is stored in an overhead bin, and you must not be so tall that you are unable to walk upright in the aircraft cabin. Although you cannot do anything to alter your height, you can identify airlines that accept applicants with your physical attributes.

Weight

Another checklist item to consider is weight. Most airlines require candidates to be within proportionate weight-to-height standards. The term "weight-to-height standards" is a bit unclear, and courts have ruled regarding the specifics of airlines' weight requirements. Airlines continue, however, to use weight tables based on height, frame, age, and gender variables.

Most of the weight tables used are variations of the weights recommended by insurance companies. Doctors, too, usually have weight charts in their offices. You should try to obtain one of these charts to use as a general guideline.

Many airlines do not identify their minimum—yes, you can be too thin—and maximum weights to prospective employees, but if you are hired you will be made aware of what weight you may not exceed or fall below. Some airlines weigh you at an interview; others just "eyeball" you, at least at your first meeting or interview.

You will be weighed several times during training and then periodically once you are flying. There are, of course, certain aesthetic reasons for these weight restrictions, whether anyone will admit it or not. The current argument for them is health-related, and many people agree that a flight attendant may not have the energy, stamina, or reaction time needed if he or she is carrying around several extra pounds.

Below is an example of a height/weight table. It is a fairly strict example and illustrates only recommended

Height	*Female Weight (lbs.)*	*Male Weight (lbs.)*
5′2″	118	130
5′3″	121	135
5′4″	125	140
5′5″	129	145
5′6″	133	150
5′7″	137	155
5′8″	141	160
5′9″	145	165
5′10″	149	170
5′11″	153	175
5′12″	157	180

weights. It does not illustrate minimum or maximum weights, nor does it allow for age or frame variations.

If your weight is a quite a bit higher than an airline's requirements, you can begin working to reach your recommended weight range. Crash dieting is not the answer. Usually, people who starve themselves either gain back all the weight they have lost or succumb to an eating disorder to maintain the weight loss. Try eating well-balanced meals and increasing your exercise time. Consult a doctor or nutritionist about creating a diet plan that allows you to lose weight in a healthy manner.

Vision

Another item on the checklist is vision. The minimum required uncorrected and corrected vision varies, but in general it is uncorrected 20/100, corrected to 20/30 or better. Glasses or contact lenses are acceptable, although the airline may place restrictions on the style of frame you may wear when in uniform. If you wear corrective lenses and the application asks whether you wear glasses or contact lenses, do not say "no" thinking that will give you an edge over other applicants. A cursory eye exam is part of the preemployment physical. Do wear your glasses to your interview if you need them. If your vision is not up to the airline's minimum standard, check with your doctor for advice. Again, do your homework; some smaller airlines may have more flexible vision requirements.

Health

Item number four is health. Most airlines require preemployment physical examinations. Some examinations are more thorough than others, but all airlines look for basically the same thing: any physical problem that might disqualify you for flight duty.

High blood pressure will disqualify you. Heart problems will disqualify you. Chronic sinus infection, back problems, hearing impairments, and certain genetic and acquired syndromes will disqualify you. If you are required to take daily prescription medications, you probably will be disqualified.

One aspect of a flight attendant career to be considered is that most of the work is performed at high altitudes, in an environment that is foreign to the human body. We are terrestrial creatures. Through research and technical engineering not only can we survive the upper reaches of the atmosphere, but it is made tolerable enough that we can spend time there in relative comfort. You should remember, however, that these are alien and hostile surroundings in which we place ourselves, and as a result our bodies are subjected to certain phenomena that are not normal.

Some conditions that are peculiar to altitude, pressurization, or high-speed travel include the following:

1. Constant exposure to near-zero humidity.
2. Occasional exposure to both positive and negative gravitational or "g" forces.
3. Desynchronosis, or jet lag, in which your internal clock is out of sync from crossing too many time zones.
4. Hypoxia, a condition in which your body does not utilize enough oxygen. (People who have vascular or circulatory problems, who have certain blood, respiratory, or cellular conditions, or who are required to use certain medications such as sulfa drugs are at much higher risk of becoming hypoxic in flight.)
5. Dysbarism, a general term encompassing several types of decompression sickness, including trapped or evolved systemic gases. (It can mean anything from a toothache resulting from

expanding air caught in a cavity to complications involving the central nervous system. Such disturbances can be common—an earache occurring when pressure cannot equalize because of blockage of the eustachian tube—or they can be extremely rare—bends or parathesia.)

You could go to work with a cold if you worked in an office, but you cannot fly with a cold. Flying with blocked sinuses leads to extreme pain and can result in eardrum rupture. Nor can you just decide that you'll swallow a decongestant to clear up your head. Most over-the-counter decongestants and antihistamines, as well as prescription medications, may not be used by pilots or flight attendants while on duty.

Other prescription and nonprescription medications that may not be used when flying include motion sickness medication, allergy medications, certain antibiotics, tranquilizers, insulin, and muscle relaxers. The list is almost endless.

Another aspect of the job to consider is the entire lifestyle. You will work nights as well as days, at times one right after the other. You will occasionally skip meals because you are too busy to eat. Sometimes you will be short on rest. In January you may fly from Minneapolis, where the temperature is below freezing, to San Juan, where it is 82°F. You may cross international borders and be exposed to differences in food and water.

The entire lifestyle of a flight attendant can cause stresses on the body. One simply must be in good health to successfully withstand the demands of working such a hectic schedule and such extreme variations in climate and diet.

Another consideration is drugs. All airline companies in the United States require, by law, preemployment drug screening, in addition to periodic random drug testing, of their safety-related employees (including flight attendants). If traces of any of the following substances are found, you will not even be considered for hire; if you are already working for an airline, you will be removed from duty:

- Marijuana
- Cocaine
- Opiates
- Phencyclidine or PCP
- Amphetamines

When taking your preemployment physical, be sure to report to the doctor any medications, prescription or over-the-counter, that you have taken during the last several weeks. Also, be sure to abstain from drinking alcohol—including in religious observance, if possible—for several days before your physical. These precautions may protect you from having questionable test results.

If you have any questions regarding your current physical condition, you should check with your family physician or your school nurse. These medical specialists should be able to discuss any physical problems and what long-term effects they may have. A doctor or nurse also can identify any other problems that may disqualify you from a flight attendant career.

Education

The fifth item on the checklist is education. You must be at least a high school graduate or have a GED. This is the minimum requirement. Most airlines, however, prefer applicants who have taken some college classes, and often they give greater consideration to applicants who have earned a college degree.

Many areas of study will prove helpful to a career as a flight attendant. Many focus on communications.

Knowledge of a foreign language can be a great asset when traveling on foreign flights or simply for communicating with foreign travelers. Asian languages—Japanese or Chinese—are useful as well as Western languages such as French and German. The ability to speak another language can make the difference in your being hired should some of your other qualifications be minimal or marginal.

Speech and general communications skills are very important for a flight attendant. If you need work in this area, you should enroll in a course to improve your skills. Public speaking skills will be useful throughout the interview process and your airline career. Interviews are conducted in a group format. You may be asked to stand before the group and give a capsule history of your life. When working on a flight, you will have to stand up in front of an entire plane of people to provide a safety briefing. Don't get caught with a dry mouth and wet hands.

Another area of education that can be a great help on the job is first aid. Enroll in a first-aid or safety course. If you are in college, take at least one pre-med course. You must learn basic first aid during your flight attendant training, and it definitely helps if you are already able to recognize the difference between diabetic coma and insulin shock.

Although since World War II it has not been a requirement of flight attendant work to be a registered nurse, if you have the time and resources you should consider it. Being a nurse is even better than speaking Japanese if you need an extra edge to get hired. Airlines love it, and you can add to your flight attendant income by working part time for a doctor or in a hospital on your days off.

Check with your local junior college to see if it offers a flight attendant program. Many do, especially in southern California. The programs can be fun, and they also give you extra preparation for your flight attendant training.

You might consider a course in gourmet food and wine. That is something you can use in your private life, and it really does help when you are in the galley of a 747 trying to figure out the difference between California Cabernet and French Beaujolais. Sometimes just trying to pronounce the food choices on a Tokyo flight can be defeating.

One important area to study is geography. You would probably find it quite embarrassing if you announced to your passengers, "Welcome to Toronto, New York," or, "We have just landed in Kitty Hawk, Arkansas." Not knowing where you are also makes it pretty hard to figure out what time zone you are in. Most domestic airlines publish their flight attendant schedules in local time. If you think you are in Mountain Time when in fact you are in Central Time, you are going to be late, and we have already discussed the undesirable results of tardiness.

Many other courses can be of benefit to you as a flight attendant. Consider a well-rounded education with emphasis on the things discussed above. Knowledge of office skills, mathematics (for figuring out time zones and foreign currency), English, history, business, and management can all prove helpful.

Remember that whatever you choose to study, your education will never be wasted. In addition to everyday use of your skills and knowledge on a flight, you may find yourself promoted more quickly. Promotions often are made on the basis of educational background.

Work Experience

Most airlines prefer applicants who have worked for two or more years in positions involving customer service.

Customer service can mean a lot of things, but typically it means that have you dealt with the public face-to-face on a daily basis—and not only survived the experience but enjoyed it. You might consider jobs in the following areas:

- Restaurants or fast-food operations
- Retail stores
- Hotels or motels
- Tourist attractions or theme parks
- Tourist operations
- Customer service departments of utilities companies
- Car rental agencies
- Conventions
- Airports
- Hospitals

Remember that it is important that you work with the public. In a job as a hotel housekeeper, you'll be working in an empty hotel room. Select a position that places you in immediate contact with people of all kinds.

It also is important that you choose a job and stick with it for a while. Do not change jobs several times a year. This says to a potential employer that you may not be looking for long-term employment.

Do remember a "good people" story, in which you helped someone in need, and a "bad people" story, in which someone was terrible to you and you dealt with him or her in a professional manner without losing your patience. You might be asked to discuss situations like these during an interview.

Age

Although the minimum age for application can be as young as 18, most carriers have a minimum age of 20 or

21, and they often prefer candidates over the age of 25. Airlines are now hiring for the long term and believe that the chances for a mutually successful relationship are best if the people they hire are more stable and mature. Age, of course, is not the only measure of maturity, but most airlines figure it's a good place to start.

No airline may legally refuse to hire you based on a maximum age. You may apply for a position until you are at the legal retirement age.

Specific Requirements

Appendix I lists specific minimum physical qualifications for a variety of airlines, but for now we will be satisfied with the general guidelines into which you must fit to be considered for a flight attendant job. Remember that requirements often change; you should ask specific airlines for an up-to-date listing of the qualifications required.

The preflight checklist is now complete. You have taken stock of your physical assets and determined what may be done to meet or exceed the minimum qualifications. You have formulated a plan for the immediate future in the areas of work experience and education, and you have resolved to improve any deficiencies in the employment profile the airlines have established for flight attendants.

Our Imaginary Airlines aircraft and crew now are ready for boarding. In the next chapter we begin our search for the right airline company, fill out applications, and go to an interview. Takeoff time is not far away.

3

Boarding: Finding the Right Airline

The airplane is clean, checked, and ready to go. The passenger service agent or gate agent has come on board and checked with the senior flight attendant and the captain to see if all is ready to receive passengers. The flight attendants assume their assigned stations for boarding.

There may be pre-boards, people who are allowed a little extra time before general boarding is announced. They may be celebrities, families traveling with small children, or others who for reasons such as age or physical challenge may need a few more minutes to get settled.

As the passengers arrive at the door of the aircraft, they are greeted by the flight attendant assigned to that position. This person is usually but not always the senior flight attendant. On certain aircraft a center door, a rear door, or even multiple doors may be used. In that case another flight attendant may be there to greet and assist passengers. As a flight attendant you need to be thoroughly familiar with the layout (also termed "configuration") of the aircraft you are working, since the most common passenger need at this point is assistance in finding seat assignments.

The flight attendants who are assigned the in-cabin boarding stations help passengers to put away or "stow" their carry-on baggage. (Most flight attendants dislike carry-on baggage because of all the federal regulations involved.) All carry-ons must be securely restrained in an overhead bin, beneath a passenger seat, or in an approved closet. With the high-density seating required to be competitive in today's marketplace, passenger seats now are installed where most of the approved closets used to be.

The limited space is a problem. Before there were regulations about the size of carry-on luggage, people tried to bring all sorts of things on board. I have seen 30″ by 40″ picture frames, piñatas, four-foot statues, bird cages (with birds), and steamer trunks all pulled, pushed, kicked, and carried down the jetway. Occasionally, someone's garment bag would be so heavy I'd swear there was a stowaway inside.

Once all the passengers are settled, a head count is taken and the doors are closed and locked. The senior flight attendant informs the captain that the "Cabin is secure" or that the flight attendants are "Ready for push-back." As a passenger, you probably have heard an announcement like, "Flight attendants prepare for departure." That is a signal from the senior flight attendant for the others to arm their doors, that is, to engage the escape slides attached to the doors. Depending on the aircraft, this may involve a flight attendant's bending down and physically securing a bar to brackets in the aircraft floor, or it simply may involve moving a lever on the door to another position. When that is accomplished, the boarding process is complete.

DECIDING WHAT YOU WANT

On this Imaginary Airlines flight, boarding includes the steps required to identify airlines for which you'd like to work. Throughout the boarding process, you will analyze which companies meet your needs, requirements, and qualifications. The first step to doing this is making a list of the job requirements that fit your needs:

1. Do you want to work on international flights or on domestic (within the United States) flights?
2. Do you want to work for a large company, or would you prefer something smaller?
3. Do you mind being based far from home and family, or would you like to be based near them?
4. What are your minimum financial and benefit-package requirements?
5. What are the airline's minimum requirements compared to your qualifications?
6. Will it be possible for you to be away for long periods of time (10 to 18 days, for example), or do you need to return to your home base each night?
7. Would you prefer to work on a jet airplane, or could you work on a small or propeller aircraft?

These questions are areas you should consider when researching possible employers. It is important that you honestly assess your wants and needs and that you try to identify an airline that best suits those needs. Accepting a job without considering these key questions would probably result in making both you and the airline unhappy with the choice.

Identifying Airlines by Type

There are several types of airline operations, including scheduled airlines, charter airlines, commuter or regional airlines, and corporate airlines. Each type of airline employs flight attendants to look after passengers' comfort and safety during a flight.

Scheduled Airlines

Major airlines such as Delta, USAir, American, and Northwest are scheduled carriers. This means that they each publish a schedule of flights and sell tickets to the general public. Tickets are sold at the airport, over the phone, at travel agencies, and at ticket offices. National airlines such as Alaska Air or Midway Airlines also are considered scheduled carriers, but their route structures, numbers of employees, and annual revenues are not as large as those of the major airlines.

Major carriers employ thousands of workers, with as many as ten thousand or more flight attendants. Because of the immense size of these organizations, employees become numbers. When you are hired you will be issued an employee number, just as the military issues a serial number to its employees. You also will be given a system seniority number and a base seniority number. Almost everything at work happens to you because of one of those numbers: You get your schedule by your base seniority number, you are paid by your employee number, and you do or do not get furloughed (laid off) by your system seniority number.

Although being a "number" may seem unappealing, working for a large organization has its benefits. The airline is better known to the public, you have a greater chance of a secure career, and you generally do get better pay and benefits. You have to decide which is more important to you. If you have to be you instead of file number 372492, you should look to a smaller air carrier for employment. If greater job security and company identification are important, you probably should begin your job search with the larger airlines.

When considering larger airlines, look at the routes each offers. Although nearly all of the major carriers have some international routes, the chance to fly them depends on a lot of factors, two of which are seniority and language ability. Sometimes airlines have separate bases for flight attendants who qualify for the international routes. If you wish to fly internationally, be sure to ask your interviewer how long you would have to wait before you would be allowed to fly out of the country with the airline. If it would be six or ten years, you may wish to consider other options.

If you want to see America first but may be required by your airline to fly internationally, you should discuss this during your interview as well.

Next, check the base or domicile locations of the airline for which you think you would like to work. For instance, you live in Seattle and want to stay there. You find that United has a base in Seattle. You're all set, right? *Wrong*. Seattle is a very senior base for UAL. The chances of your being assigned there out of training are almost nonexistent. A base opening occurs when someone transfers out, resigns, or retires, or when the airline changes its route structure to include additional equipment that will be staffed from that location. When all on-file transfer requests have been honored from those who are already flying and an opening remains, then, and only then, will that base be open to the Training Center. If such a situation should arise, the base assignments are then awarded on the basis of class seniority, which is discussed in Chapter 4. Of course, stranger things have happened, but I would plan to spend a few years in New York or Cleveland.

If propellers make you nervous, go to work for a major carrier. With the exception of America West, they do not have any. Some nationals like Air Wisconsin have mixed fleets, and commuter/regional airlines fly propeller aircraft almost exclusively. If you do not know what an aircraft is simply by a letter/number description, ask the interviewer. Here are some examples:

Jets	*Props*
DC-10	DC-3
BAe-146	BA-3101
DC-8	DHC-8
F-100	F-27
A-320	ATR-42
MD-80	EMB-120
B-767	SD3-60

Confused? I don't blame you. Sometimes even I get confused. So ask.

Stability is a relative term when relating to employment, especially in the airline industry. If you choose a major or national airline, chances are pretty good that it will be around ten years from now. However, as a seniority number, you should know the rest of the story. The number of employees a company keeps on its payroll has to do with the economic upturns and downswings. When things get tight in the marketplace, we have a furlough situation; that means you get laid off. The process starts at the bottom and works its way up the seniority list. This situation can last from a few weeks to several years, depending on the state of the economy. A furloughed employee always is recalled before a new hiring takes place, but by then you may not care.

Then there is the merger/acquisition scenario to consider. In such a situation the seniority lists are usually merged. This does not happen on a one-to-one basis. Actually, a 12-to-1 ratio is considered good. The dominant partner gets twelve seniority numbers for each one of the other partner. If Imaginary Airlines buys See America Airlines and you are number one on the latter's flight attendant seniority list, you end up number 13 on the merged list, number two ends up number 26, three at 38, and so on. You can probably live with that if you do happen to be number one. If not, you may end up bumped out of your domicile or, worse yet, squeezed off the bottom.

There are several other ways, generally not even this good, in which company personnel are shuffled when mergers or acquisitions occur. Just going to work for a large airline is not in itself a ticket to job security. The forecast is that you have a good chance of holding on to your job and that prospects are favorable for expansion and profitability in the next ten years.

As for opportunity for promotion, it is not necessarily best with a large company. When openings occur, they are posted for application. You must apply in writing, and if you meet the minimum qualifications you will be interviewed. You rarely will be promoted to a managerial position without a college degree, but you may win rotation positions, such as to the training staff, by your merit, record, and ability. The fact is that most flight attendants would rather not bother in the first place. Not that they are not ambitious, but they generally have it much better where they are, and they know it. When you add up seniority raises, days off, per diem, and incentive pay, you make a lot more money on the line and you don't have to put up with office politics five days a week. If the carrier is union, promotion to a supervisory position may necessitate surrendering your seniority number, which means that you cannot go back to flying if there are staff cutbacks or you decide the job is not for you. The situation is surely worth thorough consideration before deciding to climb corporate ladders in this business.

Charter Airlines

Some airline carriers focus exclusively on the charter market. This type of airline does not sell tickets to individual members of the public; instead it sells tickets to groups and tour operators who contract for the entire aircraft on a specific day to go to a specific place. If a tour operator contracts the aircraft, he or she may then place advertisements in the newspapers or magazines offering to sell seats on what is called a public charter. Since all of these charter trips are sold well in advance, as a flight attendant you have a monthly schedule. But no schedule is published in the Official Airline Guide (OAG) or available at airport ticket counters.

In the "old days" we used to call these airlines "supplemental" or "non-sched" carriers. They were at the same time the best and the worst for which to work. They were terrible because flight attendants often were abused with excessive duty hours well past the limits of human endurance. Sometimes they flew for days without sleep or a bath. I remember stories about planes taking off with flight attendants hysterically beating their fists against the doors begging to be let out.

They were the best because they were the most fun. While I was at United flying to such ordinary ports as Muskegon, Flint, and Moline, they were having week-long layovers in Paris, Athens, and Rome. When I got to Grand Rapids for my big twelve-hour RON, my crew, whose names I barely knew, ran to their rooms and did the old "Slam-Click" routine. That's the sound of the door slamming and the lock clicking into place. By contrast, the charter crews were like family. They lived on the road together, had fun together, worked together, and cared about each other in a way that major airline crews, because of the vast numbers of personnel employed, never could. Because I was lucky enough to work with some of these non-scheders in my later career, I found out what the crew concept was all about and was able to build many friendships that remain fresh and warm through all the years and distances that separate us.

Does that kind of thing still happen? Yes and no. Duty abuses are no longer as common and with some charter carriers do not happen at all. The crew closeness is still much more in evidence than with major carriers because of the free time you spend together in faraway places (layovers may be several days long) and because the companies are smaller.

I do recommend that charter airlines be seriously considered as an option, especially if you want to fly all over the world immediately, do not mind being away for up to three weeks, and would like to be a name instead of a number. American Trans Air is the biggest and the best, with a consistently good record in all areas.

A word of caution—*do* research the companies thoroughly. Many have wonderful reputations and happy employees, but there also are some that are not so terrific. The best thing to do is talk to flight attendants who work for the airline you are considering.

Since most charter operators are very small, long-term stability often is not good. Many of the airlines that have disappeared in the last ten years have been charters. You'll have a great time while it lasts, but you may end up on a merry-go-round of unemployment, company bankruptcy, and lost benefits.

Commuter/Regional Airlines

A third alternative for employment is the commuter or regional carrier. If the idea of working on a megaplane or for a megaconglomerate makes you uncomfortable, you may want to focus on something smaller and closer to home that still retains the advantages of identity with a major carrier. Most regionals have entered into code share agreements with a major airline. Some regionals are owned by the parent company of a major air carrier. An example of this is American Eagle and American Airlines, which are owned by AMR Corp. Other airlines, like United Express Carriers and United Airlines/UAL Inc., have only a business agreement between them.

Although scheduled, the regional airlines are much smaller than their big brothers, so you are able to meet people more easily. You are often the only flight attendant on the aircraft and therefore can have more personal contact with your passengers. Most of your trips are structured to have you home almost every night, and the bases are usually in smaller cities, perhaps even in your own hometown. The airplanes are smaller and slower, and you never have to learn complicated meal services. The training does not take as long, so you are able to go to work and start earning sooner. Some people choose a regional to try out their vocation, hoping to change to a major after they have learned the ropes. Many do go on to larger carriers, but some people like it so much that they stay forever.

The disadvantages of working for a regional are generally lower pay and longer working hours. You will never fly international. You will never fly a 747 except on vacation. You fly at lower altitudes where the air is not always smooth.

On the other hand, you will not get jet lag, fly an eighteen-hour leg, or have to go to the Middle East. It does not matter if you do not speak French, cannot open a bottle of champagne without spilling, or would rather spend a cozy night at home than try to figure out the dinner menu in Madrid.

Employment stability is generally good, and the same rules apply as on the large airlines: When people stop flying, they trim their payrolls. If times are good, you work.

Chances for promotion are excellent because people

get to know you by the job you do. You may even be offered a position you had no idea was available, and the pay will probably be better than what you were making. However, people are people, and you still have to put up with the office pecking order five days a week.

Corporate Airlines

Most corporate flight attendants have gained experience by working for one of the three types of airlines discussed above. Some corporate airline departments do hire without previous experience, and you should be aware that such jobs exist. If you think you might be interested in this type of flying, you should visit your local library and check company directories for listings of corporations that have separate airline divisions. Once you've identified these companies, you can call or write for a list of qualifications. Be aware, however, that this type of flying is big business and very, very hard work. You have to convey the image of being equally at home in the boardroom and the crewroom, and you may need gourmet cooking and serving references, or possibly secretarial skills as well.

Some entertainers also own private jets and may pick up flight attendants from a corporate crew-leasing pool on occasion. This can be exciting work, but you should consider that you may be required to be away from home for excessively long periods of time. Flight attendants for corporate airlines often travel for weeks at a time, and sometimes they are away for months. The financial rewards for this type of work, however, are excellent.

Learning More About Specific Airlines

Once you have decided which type of operation you would prefer, you should begin to research individual airlines. You need to check each airline's minimum qualifications against your qualifications. Look at the requirements for minimum age, height, weight, education, language ability, and employment experience. Specifics for some airlines are listed in Appendix I. If your airline choice is not listed there, look up its address in The World Aviation Directory, which is available at most public libraries.

Whether or not your airline is listed in the appendix, you should write the airline for more information. Request information on minimum qualifications, domiciles, equipment, salary scales, and route structure. Most major and national airlines have brochures that will answer all these questions and more.

As you learn more about your airline choices, match the specifics with your requirements. Be sure to choose several airlines to research. Many successful flight attendants working today were not hired by their first choice. If these men and women had limited themselves to one airline only, they could have ruined their chances to have rewarding flight attendant careers.

APPLYING TO AIRLINES OF CHOICE

There are two ways to apply for a job with an airline. The first is the easiest: Check the classified section of your local paper for airlines that are doing field recruiting. With field recruiting, airline representatives visit a city and interview a large number of applicants. By participating in field recruiting, you can shave months off the hiring process. Presenting yourself in person is the fastest way to get hired.

Another way to apply for a job is to send an airline your résumé. Most major airlines will return your résumé to you with an application form. Some airlines will keep it on file. Others, especially small airlines, accept only résumés and use them as a basis for informing candidates of interview opportunities.

Cover Letters and Résumés

When preparing a cover letter and résumé, there are a number of things to consider:

First: Do not spend money on a fancy professional résumé that comes with a cookie-cutter-format cover letter. Everyone knows where you got it, and that doesn't say a lot for your originality or creativity.

Second: Develop a cover letter of your own. Request an application for a job as a flight attendant and say that you are enthusiastic about the possibility of working for a carrier like this one and why. For Pete's sake, make it sound sincere and personal. Enclose a copy of your résumé.

It will benefit you in the long run to compose an original letter for each airline. The person receiving it may even read it and be impressed enough to make sure you get an interview, or at least the application. You may wish to choose a good bond paper in a shade other than white, perhaps cream or very light blue. Do not use dark or Day-Glo shades. With the thousands of résumés and letters received each month by each airline, it certainly does not hurt to stand out a little, provided it is done in good taste.

Third: Type or word-process the cover letter and résumé, even if you have to borrow a machine or use the library's. Be sure the paper is clean, the spelling is correct, and that you have no typos. Neatness does count!

Fourth: The résumé. One page only, please; two at most. *Do not* send copies of twelve letters of reference; save those for the interview. *Do not* sent a photograph unless specifically requested to do so. *Do not* state your age, weight, personal status, or gender except what may be deduced from your name. *Do not* indicate your national origin, race, or religious affiliation.

Do something like this:

NAME
STREET ADDRESS
CITY, STATE, ZIP
AREA CODE, TELEPHONE NUMBER

Position Desired:	Flight Attendant
Professional Experience:	most recent next recent next recent etc.
Education:	Degree received or years attended: Graduate School/course of study College or University/course of study Junior College/course of study Technical, Business, or Trade School/course of study Adult Extension Courses/subjects taken High School/diploma or GED
Talent or Ability:	Languages spoken/written/read Lived in another country
Outside Activities:	Volunteer work in related fields; e.g., hospital/senior home, etc. Scout Leader

Willing to relocate at company discretion.
Personal and professional references upon request.

That's all there is to it. This type of résumé and cover letter will give you as good a chance as anyone else, or better. If your résumé is returned, an application will come with it. That simply means that it is not company policy to accept résumés. You may receive a letter saying that your résumé will be kept on file for six months, or you may hear nothing.

Do not be discouraged. That's just the way some companies do things. *Do* keep a written log of all your correspondence, the date it was sent, and the reply. You may need to resubmit your résumé or application after six months or a year. If you have not been hired by then, do so.

After copies of your résumé and cover letter have been mailed, continue to search for new opportunities while you wait for replies. Keep checking newspapers and magazines. Try scanning the trade publications, magazines, or newsletters that focus on the aviation community. These can be excellent sources of information by identifying who is hiring, by listing locations where interviews are held, and by discussing what new carriers are starting operations.

Some of these publications can be quite expensive, so you may want to check your local public or college library first. Some libraries in your area may collect books and materials dealing with different aspects of aviation. Visit these to collect information.

Airline Applications

The mailbox is starting to overflow with all the wonderful correspondence you have been waiting for! You open the envelopes with cautious care and a pounding heart only to find—*applications. Big, long, applications.* Never fear, we can handle that.

Applications are of two kinds: one specifically for flight attendants, and a more general one for all positions. Following is an example of the flight attendant application. You must either print or type it. If you choose to print, use black ink. First have the application copied to use as a rough draft so you can practice. Be sure of your information beforehand. All addresses, telephone numbers, and references will be checked. Again, neatness counts. If it cannot be easily read, they will probably not bother to try.

FLIGHT ATTENDANT APPLICATION
IMAGINARY AIRLINES

General Instructions: Read the terms of employment carefully. Print or type the answers to every question. If a question does not apply, indicate by N/A. All information in this application will be treated confidentially except where permission for release of such information is provided by the Flight Attendant Applicant Agreement. Employment with the company is dependent upon the truthfulness and completeness of the information provided by you in this application.

PERSONAL DATA

Last Name, First Name, Middle Name Date

Present Address Telephone/Home

Permanent Address Telephone/Business

If address is small town or suburb, state nearest city served by Imaginary Airlines: ____________

In case of emergency notify: Name
Address

Social Security # U.S. citizen? If no, date of entry
Yes No Alien Registration #

Have you ever been convicted of violating a law? (Do not list traffic violations.) Yes _____ No _____

If yes, please attach, on a separate sheet of paper, an explanation of the conviction and the circumstances surrounding the conviction. Disclosure of a conviction does not disqualify you automatically from further employment consideration. Each case will be considered separately. However, falsification or omission of information relating to a conviction will result in your immediate dismissal from employment with this company.

Have you ever been interviewed for any position with this company? Yes _____ No _____ When _____ Where _____ Position _____

Have you ever attended Flight Attendant Training for this company? Yes _____ No _____ Year _____ Class _____

Do you have any relatives employed by this company? Yes _____ No _____
If yes, identify individual(s) and relationship(s). _______

Have you ever been employed by this company? Yes _____ No _____
If yes, provide dates of employment. _________________

Have you ever held a security clearance? Yes ___ No ___
If yes, state where granted and type of clearance. ______
Have you ever been bonded? Yes ________ No ________
If yes, state where and by what employer. _____________
Have you ever been refused a bond? Yes _____ No _____
If yes, when and why? _____________________________
____

CHARACTER REFERENCES

Do not refer to mere acquaintances, previous employers, or relatives. List people whom you know well either personally or in business.

Name Occupation Address/Telephone Number

____

____

____

____

PHYSICAL DATA

Measurements: Height __________ Weight __________

Is your vision corrected/uncorrected at least 20/30 in each eye? Yes _____ No _____

Time lost through illness in past two years __________

Nature of illness ______________________________

____

WORK INTEREST

How soon can you report for training? _____ Notice required? _____

Are you willing to work nights, weekends, and holidays? Yes _____ No _____

Are you willing to relocate? Yes _____ No _____

EDUCATION

List all schools attended

High School	Name and Address of School	Dates Attended	Graduated Yes or No	Degree Major
College or University				
Graduate School				
Business or Technical				

Circle the languages you speak fluently:
English French Spanish German Japanese
Portuguese Italian Chinese Other: ______________

____

EMPLOYMENT RECORD

List all previous work experience including military service and periods of unemployment. Begin with present position and work back to your first position. Attach résumé if necessary. If there were periods of more than one month in which you were self-employed or unemployed, list the name and address of person(s) who can verify your activities. *Failure to accurately complete this application may disqualify you from consideration.*

Employer Address/ Telephone Number	Dates of Employment Start/End	Salary Start/ Ending	Job Title and Description	Specific Reason for Leaving

STANDARD FLIGHT ATTENDANT APPLICANT AGREEMENT

I hereby authorize and request each person, firm, or corporation listed on my application to answer questions that may be asked by Imaginary Airlines and to give any information that may be sought by this company concerning this application, me, or my work habits, character, or skills. I also authorize Imaginary Airlines to furnish information to others relative to my record in the Inflight Training Center. I will submit to examination by physicians of the company's selection as often as may be requested and also will submit to such examination in connection with any claim against the Training Center.

The Inflight Recruitment Office will advise me in writing if I have been selected for enrollment in the Training Center. Due to the large number of interviews, if an applicant has not heard within 90 days of the interview s/he can presume s/he was not selected for enrollment. If selected for enrollment, I understand that I will not be considered an employee of the company during the time I am enrolled. The privileges, if any, which may accrue to me as an employee of the company will become effective in accordance with the company's rules and regulations and the union contract. I understand that I need to bring sufficient funds to care for my personal needs while enrolled at the Training Center. The company, however, will furnish room, board, and classroom equipment during my enrollment at the Training Center.

I agree and understand that I may be dismissed from the Training Center at the sole discretion of the company, at any time, without any advance notice, and without, except as provided herein, any liability to me on the part of the company. I understand that the company reserves the right to alter the size of the training class, to change the starting or completion dates of a training class, or to cancel a training class at any time.

Should I be dismissed from the Training Center for reasons beyond my control, I will be reimbursed for out-of-pocket expenses not to exceed the rate of $— per day for every day I was enrolled at the Training Center, plus those additional expenses incurred by me at the specific direction of the Training Center. Further, in such an instance, I will be provided with transportation, by the most practical means, back to the point from which I initially proceeded to the Training Center.

I understand that 60 days after my assignment to a base station as a flight attendant, I will be required, as a condition of my continued employment, to maintain membership in the Association representing the flight attendants for purposes of the Railway Labor Act, to the extent of paying the initial fee and membership dues.

Furthermore, I agree that:

1. My employment shall be in accordance with the terms of (A) this application, (B) company rules and regulations and any amendments thereto, and (C) any applicable labor agreement. The company will have the right to amend, modify, and revoke its rules and regulations at any time. I will familiarize myself promptly with such rules and regulations and will abide by and be bound by the rules and regulations now and hereafter in effect.

2. My employment may be terminated by the company at any time without advance notice, its only obligation being to pay wages or salary earned by me to the date of my termination. Without limitation, my failure to abide by rules and regulations, my failure to pass a company physical examination related to my job requirements, and my falsification or omission of any information in this application will entitle the company to terminate my employment. No other representation concerning my employment with the company has been made to me. I understand that any such other representation, to be binding upon the company, must be authorized in writing by an officer of the company.

3. I will submit to medical examination(s) by a physician appointed by the company at such time(s) as it may request, and will submit to such examination in

connection with any claim against the company for injuries suffered during the course of my employment.

4. I agree that my employment is contingent upon my meeting all placement considerations, including appropriate medical requirements.

5. I agree that all right, title, and interest, including without limitation all copyrights and patents, in and to any material produced or inventions developed by me, which affect or relate to the company's business or which affect or relate to the air transportation industry, will vest in the company and that I will have no personal right, title, or interest whatsoever therein.

6. The company, and any person or concern it may authorize, is entitled, without my further consent, to copyright, sell, or use in any manner any picture or photograph of me.

7. The company has the right, at any time after the termination of my employment, to furnish to others information concerning my employment history with the company, including the information contained in this application.

8. I agree not to disclose any of the company's trade secrets or other confidential or restricted information and not to make unauthorized use of any such trade secrets or other confidential or restricted information in any fashion during my employment or after the termination of my employment with the company.

9. I consent to any search by the company representatives of property owned by me, or within my custody or control, which may be reasonably required to protect the company's interest. I agree to cooperate in any company investigation by giving true and complete answers to all questions and by complying with all other requests for assistance and information.

10. This is to inform you that as part of the procedure for processing your employment application, an investi-

gative consumer report may be prepared whereby information is obtained through personal interviews with your neighbors, friends, or others with whom you are acquainted. This inquiry includes information as to your character, general reputation, personal characteristics, and mode of living. You have the right to make a written request within a reasonable time to receive additional, detailed information about the nature and scope of this investigation.

________ 19________ ______________________
Date Signature of applicant in ink

It is vital to you that you do several things in preparation for filling out an airline application:

1. Keep an accurate record of dates of employment, school attendance, and military service if applicable.
2. Keep a current address book with the following:
   a. School names, addresses, and telephone numbers.
   b. Employer names, addresses, and telephone numbers.
   c. Personal reference names, addresses, and telephone numbers.
3. Keep a record of your passport number if you have one, your social security number, and if applicable your alien registration number.

For the most part, the only intimidating thing about the application is the time involved to complete it and the thoroughness required in following the instructions. When you finish, there should be *no* blank spaces.

Anything that does not apply to you should be marked N/A.

It is federal law that airlines complete a written confirmation of background for prospective employees for at least five years previous to hire.

If you have not filled out an application before you are interviewed, you will be asked to do so at that time. Do not be caught without the information you will need.

Before we move on to the interview, we need to discuss briefly the Applicant Agreement, which you will almost always find in one form or another at the end of the application. The example given earlier is typical of the Agreement found on an application of a major airline. Others may not be so extensive or restrictive, but you must understand what it is that you are signing. These are legal agreements written by airline attorneys and may be hard to interpet at first glance, but by placing your signature on the application you state your understanding of and agreement to all the terms and conditions stipulated therein for a period of probably forever. Later is a heck of a time to find out that you can't live with it.

The first thing you are doing is giving the airline authority to release your employment record to anyone. The second thing is authorizing them to obtain information about you from any source you have listed on the application. You also agree to submit to a physical examination at any time the company requests it.

The company then divests itself of any obligation to you as a trainee or prospective employee if it finds out that it has overhired or suffers financial reverses and needs to cancel training while you are there. In this case only it will offer you a modicum of financial reimbursement, but it will not compensate you for the job or schooling you have left to accept a training position with the company. You will not be compensated at all should you fail to pass or for any other reason such as weight or conduct be dismissed from the program.

If a carrier has a union shop, as most major airlines do, you will be required either to join the union or to pay the initiation fees and dues for benefits derived as if you were a member. If you refuse, you will be fired. Believe it or not, this is entirely legal.

You agree to familiarize yourself with and to abide by all current and future rules and regulations of the company; noncompliance results in termination.

You agree that there will be no financial redress upon termination except for wages owed; that is, no severance pay in lieu of notice.

I cannot imagine what "trade secrets" one airline might have from another, with the possible exception of advance photos illustrating a new service or uniform design; but you agree to secrecy in that event. You also agree to keep restricted material restricted. This applies to certain security procedures you will be taught in training.

If you are asked to participate in any publicity assignments on behalf of your airline, any resulting photos become the property of the company, meaning that you cannot later claim compensation for their using you in, for instance, a commercial or an advertisement.

You agree to have your suitcase or other personal possessions inspected by the company at any time without benefit of a search warrant. This usually is not done without cause, but it can happen on a random basis.

Finally, you give the company permission to speak to anyone of their choosing by telephone or in person to ask questions about you.

If you are disturbed by any of that, do not sign the

agreement. If you do not sign, however, you will not be hired. If you have a real problem with any of the terms or conditions of employment, you will be better off in the long run knowing it up front. The larger the company you work for, the more regimentation. The rules are the rules, after all, and if you cannot abide the regulations as well as abide by the regulations, you have no place here.

One last word about the application. To save you from a nasty surprise later, I must warn you that five or six airlines charge fees for processing your application. The fees range from $10 to $25 and must be included in the form of personal check or money order to the company. Read the instructions carefully. If no fee is mentioned, no fee is expected. If a fee is expected and you need to have it waived, see if there is a way to enclose a written statement of your circumstances. If not, forget that airline and choose another. Be aware that a processing fee does not guarantee you an interview or anything else other than that your application will pass through the channels of the Inflight or Human Resources Department according to that company's established procedure.

THE INTERVIEW

Let's talk about the interview. You may be informed of an airline's preliminary interest and intent to interview you by letter, telephone call, or both. You generally are given sufficient time to prepare, in some cases two weeks to a month. Smaller and charter operators may wish to see you on only one day's notice, so be prepared.

Preparation should consist of keeping a folder containing the following:

1. A copy of your birth certificate
2. Your passport, if you have one

3. A copy of your résumé
4. The list of dates and the address book you have put together for application purposes
5. Copies of any letters of reference you may have
6. Your alien registration and U.S. work permit (green card) if applicable
7. Your Social Security card.

This folder should always be accessible, current, and ready to go with you on any interview.

Bring a good ink pen. If you have not yet filled out an application, you will be asked to do so at the interview. In any case, you will be asked to complete some form of paperwork, and it does not say much for you if you need to borrow a pen or a telephone book.

Have ready the clothing you will wear to the interview, cleaned and pressed. Keep it in a special place in your closet where it will not get wrinkled or soiled. There are several schools of thought on what type of clothing should be worn to the interview. Some consultants insist on navy blue. While there is certainly nothing wrong with a navy blue suit, as far as I know no airline has ever failed to hire anyone because of not wearing one, nor has any airline hired anyone simply because of sporting the old tried and true.

Do consider the following:

Women: The key words are conservative and in good taste. Conservative business apparel, consisting of suit, dress, or skirt, blouse, and blazer. Bright prints or patterns should be avoided. You may wish to consider lightweight clothing, as you may be weighed at the interview and not all companies allow poundage for clothes. You must wear hose and heels. Make sure your shoes are clean and in good repair. Your legs should be smoothly shaved. Take an extra pair of stockings with you in case of runs or snags. Jewelry and makeup should be understated and seek to enhance your clothes and features rather than be an attraction on their own. Hats and gloves are no longer necessary. Hair may be worn up, down, or pulled back, long or short. The color must be natural-looking. Fad hairdos are a no-no. Nails must be clean and manicured. Do not wear nail polish colors that clash with or detract from your clothing, and *no* chips are allowed. Although nail polish is not required at an interview, your hands will be scrutinized for nail cleanliness, cuticle health, and smoothness. Do not wear fake nails that might fall off at an inopportune time, and be sure the length of your nails is uniform and not too long. Do not carry an overstuffed purse. Take a hanky, just in case, and any makeup you may need for repairs. Refrain from wearing perfume; you will not wish to clash with that of others interviewing at the same time or to overwhelm your interviewer. If you have the opportunity, stop at the restroom on your way in to check your makeup. Check your teeth for telltale signs of your lunch (I sincerely hope you have eaten something. Tummy noises are embarrassing!) Freshen your lipstick. Take a deep breath. Relax!

Men: Same deal. If you skipped the preceding, go back and read it; some parts apply to you. Wear a suit or slacks with a sport coat. Be sure you do not have a big bulge in your hip pocket if that is where you carry your wallet. Wear a long-sleeved shirt and a tie. Shoes should be shined and both shoes and dress socks in good repair. Hair must be clean and trimmed, not longer than the shirt or coat collar. The same goes for sideburns and facial hair; sideburns trimmed to extend no lower than the bottom of the earlobe, mustache trimmed above the upper lip and no wider than the mouth. Be sure your nails are clean, trimmed, and buffed and your hands are spotless. Forget your after-shave just this once. No earrings; only a ring, tie tack, or cufflinks are acceptable.

You now know what to take and what to wear, but you are not quite ready yet. One more phase of preparation must be completed before the big day: the mental preparation. Do not be caught short in this area. You could have everything else perfect and still blow it here. Carefully consider the following:

1. What do you want this company to know about you?
2. What do you want to know about this company?

Think about those two questions long and hard, because they are the keys to the entire interview. I shall give you some standard interview scenarios to show you what I mean.

The Standard First Interview

Interviews may be conducted in a variety of places: in airport briefing rooms, in hotel suites or conference rooms, in airline headquarters interview rooms or offices. Be sure you know where you are going well in advance.

If the interview is in your home town or city, make a dry run to see how long it takes to get there with time to spare. *You may not be late for your interview* and still expect to be hired, no matter how good your excuse.

It the interview is in another city, take the notice you were sent with instructions. Do not trust your memory. If you are lost or confused in a strange airport, seek out a representative of the airline with which you are interviewing and ask for help. Have enough money with you to cover emergencies such as cab fares. Check the weather report on the evening before you leave. If it is 80 degrees in San Diego where you live, it may be freezing rain and in the 30s in Denver where you are interviewing. Take a raincoat, an umbrella, and an extra pair of shoes. Even if you are supposed to be home that evening, pack a small tote or overnight bag in case the freezing rain turns into a blizzard and the airport closes before you are finished with your interview. In such a case, the airline may put you up at a hotel, but you may just as likely be on your own. Have a credit card or enough cash to get a room and make your long-distance calls. Situations like this can and do happen. How you handle yourself in difficulty may make the difference in being hired. No one will ask you to explain your appearance no matter what the weather or other circumstances that have contributed to it. It will be assumed that you are always in a state of flustered disarray, and you will simply be passed over.

You have arrived at the interview location, early, perfect, and prepared. You will probably sign in with a representative of the Inflight Department or a receptionist and be given several papers to fill out and some material to read. Remember, from the moment you walk in the door you are being watched by someone, even if it is only the other interviewees. Everyone is sizing up the competition and figuring their own chances. *Do not let this intimidate you.* You have been preparing for this for a long time, and that gives you the edge. You would be amazed at how many people you will meet at an interview who have no idea what being a flight attendant is all about—people who saw an ad in yesterday's newspaper and came on a lark or just because they need a job—any job.

You look around, and then it happens: You see one or two incredibly gorgeous, impeccably well put together people. Your heart sinks. *Stop that right now*!

So what? There will be enough positions for those qualified, and as trite as it sounds, looks are not everything. I have seen airlines turn down those movie-star types because they have an underdeveloped personality or the brains of an insect. But then again . . . someone else may think you are the movie star. Think about that for a while. Second, if the model is hired, it is because he or she deserves to be and will likely turn out to be a wonderful person as well as your best friend when you *both* go to training. Take another deep breath. Relax!

Now you have become familiar with the competition, filled out your papers, read your other papers, and are looking for something to keep you occupied. What should you do? Well, for heaven's sake, do not light a cigarette or put a stick of gum in your mouth. Do not choose this time to repair your nail polish. Do not pull out this month's fashion or sports magazine. What you should do is talk to people. One airline, as part of the interview, actually asks what you know about the other candidates who were in the waiting room with you. They find that your answer helps them to tell whether you are friendly, outgoing, confident, and generally interested in other human beings.

I shall not kid you, the competition for flight attendant jobs is very stiff. Of the airlines surveyed, the averages come out something like this: Among regional airlines about 30 percent of applicants were chosen to interview, and 30 percent of those interviewed were awarded flight attendant training positions. Most major and national carriers did not have statistics on the percentage of applicants interviewed, but they did tell me that of those who were interviewed, only 5 to 6 percent were chosen for training positions.

The numbers may not be favorable, but remember all the things you have going for you. You will never get what you want if you do not take the chance. Perhaps your very first interview will be the one, or you may have to attend several before you are successful.

There are also many variables over which you have no control and of which most people are not even aware. One of those variables is the "image" an airline wants its flight attendants to project. The image may be the "girl or boy next door," the sophisticated "jet-setter," or perhaps "the intellectual." These images cannot be perceived at an interview, nor will you ever find them published. The only clues may be the publicity and advertising featuring flight attendants for a particular company. If you travel by air, choose a different carrier each time and talk to the flight attendants. Compare the similarities of appearance and manner in the crew of one airline and those that seem common to the crew of another. That will give you a clue to what a particular airline is trying to achieve. Remember, the flight attendants are the most prominent representatives of the company in its dealings with the flying public.

Interviews are similar but different. Learn from each one and take your experiences to the next. Your time is never wasted if you have gained insight. You may just project the wrong image for a particular company. Do not try to change what you are; rather find the company whose image you do fit.

Up to this point, you have probably played your coming interview over and over in your head countless times, without really knowing what to expect. You may have pictured yourself in a luxurious private office, chatting happily with someone who is a cross between Joan Collins playing Alexis and your mother. I suppose that could happen, but the chances are about as remote as a tidal wave in Kansas.

What you are most likely to find is one of the harsher facts of life. All those other people sitting in the waiting room will be moved as a group into a larger room. This is it. You are on, and I do mean ON: lights, curtain, orchestra. I have heard group interviews referred to as "animation tests." You are swimming in a fishbowl with five to thirty others, and tadpoles get eaten. No one in that room has the time or inclination to calm your fears or draw you out of your shell. You may face one interviewer or a panel consisting of executives, Human Resources persons, Inflight Department managers or supervisors, and recuiting personnel. They will be introduced to you but may not all take an active part in the interview. What they will all do is write. That will drive you crazy. It is probably designed to. Personally, I think at least half of them are composing grocery lists or doodling flowers.

Be that as it may, what it all boils down to is this: If all candidates meet the minimum requirements, if all equal opportunity regulations are in compliance, and if the interview process is standardized, in the final analysis it is simply gut instinct on the part of the interviewers that makes the decision. You will be selected if they like you and feel that hiring you is in the best interests of the company.

That's it in a nutshell. You have to figure out a way to make them like you.

Back to the fishbowl. What can you expect to happen? Any number of things, actually. Everyone has their own way of doing things. In some airlines the interviewers follow procedures that have been developed by psychological and Human Resources consulting firms.

One airline uses a series of video scenarios and a test that is graded on answers designed to ascertain your orientation to a customer-service profession.

In an interview for another company I saw twenty people seated in a semicircle facing a team of interviewers behind a long table. There was nothing in front of you, and all articles had to be placed on the floor.

This left the applicant with no defensive barriers. Observation of posture, poise, and body language was obviously a strong consideration to this company's evaluation process.

In yet another instance, I saw thirty-three people jammed into a room. The entire individual participation of each person was being called upon to stand and speak about himself or herself for a few minutes.

I have seen candidates asked to describe themselves in one word. I have seen free-for-all questions tossed into the air to see who answered, how they answered, and whether they were pushy or polite in doing so.

I also have seen some dirty tricks such as purposely keeping candidates waiting for a disgraceful length of time and observing the waiting room for signs of complaint or impatience; leaving articles around the reception room to see if someone takes them; checking the waiting room to see if someone left trash not in the proper receptacle; planting undercover personnel in the waiting room to listen to conversation. One airline that does not hire smokers places you in a room well supplied with ashtrays and then observes who lights up. You will never be hired and never know why.

In all fairness, most airlines do not practice these kinds of dirty tricks, and you would probably not want to work for one that did. My point is simply that you should be on your best behavior from the time you set foot in the door until the time the process is completed and you are headed home.

In the interview preparation, I asked you to consider the following:

1. What do you want this company to know about you?
2. What do you want to know about this company?

No matter what form the interview takes, in one part you have to find an opportunity to convey to the interviewer what you want known about you in the clearest, most concise, and sincerest way possible.

The other part of the group interview will always consist of a question and answer period. That is the time to find out anything you are still not sure about; you may not have another chance.

Do not monopolize the conversation in either part of the interview. Do *talk*. If you don't, you may come and go unnoticed. When you have the floor, try to get across as many as possible of your strongest assets for the job. Talk about your language abilities, your work experience, your appropriate education. *Smile, smile, smile*! Make eye contact with the interviewer or the panel. Look up, not down. Be confident in word and deed. Speak loud enough to be heard. Do not use slang. Be alert for an opportunity to shine. Pay attention. Finally, *smile, smile, smile*.

Even as well prepared as you are at this point, I cannot guarantee that you will be selected for a second interview. Each company has its own criteria over and above the minimum. However, if you have followed my advice so far and not yet been successful, *keep trying*. Your day will come!

One unpleasant thing that may happen is that the airline will announce names at the end of the first interview of those whom they want to remain for further processing. This is defeating and disappointing if you are not among those chosen, but at least you are spared the misery of waiting for the phone call or the letter that may never come. Do not show distress in public at not being selected. That merely reinforces the decision of the panel that you lack the qualities they are seeking. It also is easy to get a bad reputation. Experience your disappointment in private for as long as it takes. Then look back on the experience objectively and consider how you may present yourself to better advantage on your next go around.

Should you be selected for further screening, the second interview may take place directly following the first, or at some time in the future. If it is to be immediately, try to take time for a restroom break, to recheck your appearance, and to get a drink of water.

Now you get to meet Alexis on a one-to-one in private. However, don't be surprised if she is a he or even the same panel that you just left and thought you would never see again.

The same rules apply as before: poise, confidence, direct answers, eye contact, and body language. *Smile*! This time will not be quite so publicly competitive, so try to let even more of your personality shine through in your conversation. This time they *will* try to set you at ease and draw you out. They want to get to know you as best they can in a short time. Let it happen. If you feel they like you, like them back. It will show, and things will generally take care of themselves from there.

Most companies, especially the large ones, do not tell you if you have been selected at this point. That is done usually by letter. You will probably be given a place and date for a physical or a time and location to report for training or both. You will be given a telephone number to call if you need to arrange for travel to the school.

Pending your reference check and the results of your physical, you have become a flight attendant trainee.

Congratulations, I knew you could do it!

4

The Safety Briefing: Flight Attendant Training

Before a plane takes off, flight attendants demonstrate the use of emergency equipment, point to the plane's emergency exits, and describe regulations that must be followed by everyone on the flight. This is formally called the *safety briefing*, but sometimes it's referred to as the "show and tell." During the safety briefing, flight attendants position themselves in the aisles and do a series of demonstrations to the accompaniment of an announcement—all aimed at getting the passengers' attention. The only people allowed to remain standing in the aisles as the plane moves away from the gate are the flight attendants. During this time, called "taxi," flight attendants can remain standing only while performing safety-related duties.

The purpose of a briefing is to educate the passengers. The briefings were designed in response to accident investigations. During one investigation, for instance, it was learned that many passengers had trouble releasing their seatbelts to escape the aircraft. Although the use of an airplane seatbelt seems straightforward to some, others found it quite difficult. The seatbelts in automobiles have a different type of catch-and-release mechanism. When there was no light and passengers were under a great deal of stress, they reverted to instinct and tried to release an airplane seatbelt as if it were a seatbelt in their automobile.

"Safety-related duties" are defined in the Federal Aviation Regulations, or FARs. FARs are laws issued by the Federal Aviation Administration (FAA) for the regulation of the aviation industry. They are written in "Parts" pertaining to the size and purpose of the airlines to which they apply. For example, general aviation is regulated by FAR Part 91; commuter or air taxi operations are regulated by FAR Part 135; and commercial operators, including all the major and national—and some regional—airlines, are regulated by FAR Part 121. In most instances, FAR Part 121 is what will concern you.

Flight attendants learn about these safety-related duties during flight attendant training. Although you probably won't be required to memorize numerical designations for the FARs, you will be required to know all FARs pertaining to flight attendants and to the aircraft cabin and passengers. Some of the subjects covered are seatbelt observance, stowage of carry-on baggage, the number of flight attendants that must be on board for various types of aircraft, safety-related passenger address announcements, oxygen requirements, the number and types of emergency equipment that must be on board, restraint systems for galley equipment, and so on. Each regulation is not difficult to learn when you consider the reasoning behind it.

The briefing must by law contain the following information:

- Location of the safety information card
- Location and type of emergency exits
- Location of the exit lights and track or pathway lighting

- Smoking regulations, if smoking is permitted at all
- Seatbelt fasten-and-release instructions and demonstration
- Location and use of emergency oxygen masks
- Location and operation of any flotation devices that are provided
- Prohibition against tampering with lavatory smoke detectors
- Location and observance of lighted signs and placards (for example, the No Smoking signs)
- How to stow carry-on baggage
- How to fasten seatbelts.

The briefing may be given either by the working flight attendants or by using a video presentation.

Following the briefing, flight attendants make a final compliance check. They make sure that all passengers' seatbelts are fastened, all carry-on items are properly stowed, no one is smoking, all tray tables and seatbacks are in the upright and locked positions, and that everything is secured according to the rules.

Many Federal Aviation Regulations focus on how to stow baggage. If a plane experiences turbulence (bumpy weather) or must abort a takeoff, its sudden movement can cause luggage to shift. It is not unusual, for example, for a plane to experience an aborted takeoff. When the pilot slams on the brakes, anything from galley equipment to carry-on baggage to passengers will move forward at the optimum speed the aircraft has reached, even though the aircraft has stopped. Anything, that is, except for items that are restrained. Accidents occur when items—and people—are not properly stowed.

Passengers often bring things aboard the plane that cause injury to others. According to the Association of Flight Attendants, at least one passenger a day sustains an injury from falling objects inside the airplane. The objects include briefcases, bags, carts, computers, typewriters, and camcorders that have been placed in overhead compartments.

FARS are designed to minimize the number of injuries that occur from falling carry-ons. Flight attendants always walk the aisles of a plane, checking to see if carry-ons are stored entirely beneath seats and making sure that the overhead compartments are locking properly.

TRAINING

Just as the flight attendants working on this Imaginary Airlines flight have taxi duties to perform as final preparation for takeoff, a newly hired flight attendant must undergo a period of intense preparations and checks before he or she can fly. This period is called flight attendant training.

Pretraining Checklist

Before you begin training, you should make a number of preparations. The pretraining checklist below includes items that you may not need to complete if you are employed by a small carrier with a shorter training period. Adjust your preparations as necessary to suit your own training circumstances.

1. Give notice to your employer.
2. Get some luggage.
3. Go clothes and accessary shopping.
4. Clear up any loose ends.
5. Call everyone and tell them where you are going
6. Go to the bank and purchase travelers checks.
7. Pack a few things every day for two weeks before you leave.
8. Assemble your important personal papers.

This pretraining checklist may seem deceptively simple.

1. *Inform your present employer as soon as you know you are leaving.* Even if only two weeks' notice is required, any extra time will help them find and train your replacement. Continue doing the best job you can. Your employer has the right to expect you to perform as well as if you were not leaving. Besides, he or she may have a reference request from your airline on the desk. Also, the long notice will give your coworkers time to throw a big farewell bash for you. This is really getting fun, isn't it?

2. *You do not need matching luggage—just a lot of it.* Training for a major carrier can take from five to six weeks. You are required to dress every day. By dress, I mean the sort of thing you wore to your interview. You also need enough personal items to last that long. There is also the possibility that your base assignment will not allow you time to go home before reporting.

It all takes a lot of room. Do not be worried about the airline transporting it. Explain to the agent when you check in that you are going to flight attendant training. If all of your luggage cannot be accommodated on your flight, they will make sure it arrives on the next. *Your* airline is already taking care of you.

3. *You will need several basic changes of clothing.* I suggest separates that can be mixed and matched for a different look. You will need dress shoes as well as at least one pair of sneakers. You will need casual dress clothes and old clothes. You will need a bathing suit. You must bring sleepwear and lots of underwear and stockings. That's not all.

In winter you will need rainwear, including boots. You will need a warm coat, especially if your training is to take place in a cold climate. Think about gloves, mufflers, earmuffs, umbrella, scarves, and thermal underthings. There is more.

You will need all of your personal cosmetics. You will need a hairdryer and manicure set. You will need a travel alarm. You will need a picture, preferably 8″ × 10″ framed, of someone or something to remind you of home. You will need hairspray or curlers or whatever you use on your hair. You will need deodorant, a razor, and Bandaids. You will need aspirin and any other medications you may require. You will need pencils and pens and your vitamins. You will want personal stationery and stamps.

You might think ahead and include a set of sheets and towels for your first apartment. A personal coffee mug will make you feel wonderful, but the rest of the furnishings can wait for later. Clearly print your name, address, and telephone number on the *inside* of your bags. If you do not yet have outside luggage tags, you can obtain them at the airport. Your name, address, and telephone number must be on them as well. You might also write, "Route to Imaginary Airlines Training Center, Chicago, Illinois" on any unused line.

4. *Do not leave without taking care of all your responsibilities.* Make a double car payment if necessary until you can give a forwarding address. The same goes for any other payments to which you are committed.

If you attend a church or club on a regular basis, inform someone in charge where you are going so they do not think that you dropped off the face of the earth.

Do not let your driver's license expire. Renew it if necessary.

Go to the dentist for a cleaning. It might be a while before you can see him again or find one in your new city.

If you take medication (remember the restrictions), have your prescriptions filled. Out-of-state prescriptions are not honored, and you would need to hunt frantically for a doctor if you ran out.

5. *Call your friends and tell them where you are going.* Most will be pleased. Some will be jealous. Forget the latter—things between you will not get better with the passage of time, no matter how hard you try. Besides, you do not need to be made to feel guilty for achieving your dream. Get addresses of your real friends so you can write them letters. Mail call is as much anticipated in a training center as it is in the army. With any luck at all, you might get yet another bon voyage party. Hey, this is great!

6. *Whatever else you forget to take to training, take money, and plenty of it.* It will buy what you forgot. Although room and board are paid for by most major carriers, you will need to pay for incidentals and any sightseeing you may wish to do in your time off. The food is usually pretty good, but sometimes you just have to go for pizza—especially if you happen to be in Chicago where they have the best in the world (no offense to New York; that's pretty good, too).

The bulk of spending comes in establishing housekeeping in your base city. Most of you will not go back home but rather somewhere completely new to you. You will need enough money to cover surface transportation costs, apartment and utilities deposits, furnishings, food, and incidentals until you receive your first paycheck. This is one of the reasons flight attendants have the reputation of living in bunches. It is much more cost-efficient to share expenses in the beginning.

7. *With so much to remember, it will be easier if you spread your packing out over a comfortable period.* Make lists. One day, carry a notebook around with you and jot down all the personal things and appliances you use every day. These are what you will need to take with you. Sort out clothing combinations and have them

washed and ironed or cleaned or repaired as necessary. Experiment with variations. Lay out accessories that match as many things as possible. Pack your clothing in plastic food bags; that helps minimize space used, keeps like things together, and drastically reduces wrinkling. Pour any cosmetic that is in a glass bottle into a plastic travel bottle. Seal that into a plastic bag.

You get the idea. The longer you give yourself to prepare, the more complete your preparation will be.

8. *Finally, assemble all the personal papers that you took to your various interviews.* You may need them for identification, or you may be asked for them in training. Do not pack them in your luggage; take them in your carry-on bag, along with your money or medication.

The Big Day

On the day you travel to your training site, you'll probably feel both nervous and excited. This is a normal reaction, and most likely your fellow trainees will feel the same way.

If you fly to a training location, you and other trainees will probably arrive at your destination airport at the same time. Usually a bus will be waiting to take everyone back to the training site.

Once you've collected your luggage and boarded the bus, relax and look around. Talk to other people on the bus. Start getting to know these people. You'll spending a lot of time together.

When you arrive at the facility, you will check in and be assigned a room and roommate(s). Your luggage will be delivered to your room, and you will be told to report that evening to a place in the building for orientation. Since school usually starts on Monday, this is most likely Sunday afternoon, so you have between now and the orientation session to relax, unpack, and get to know your new roomies.

Orientation probably will be scheduled for early evening before dinner, because without orientation you don't know where to find the food. Maybe you should pack an apple in your carry-on—just in case.

Whoever is responsible for the trainees' health and safety while at the school conducts the briefing. In the olden days it was the housemother. That title has probably changed to reflect today's attitudes, but it is most likely the same type of person.

You will be given a book or papers with a map of the facility, times when meals are served, instructions on what to do if you get sick, pages and pages of house and school rules, dress codes, class times and locations, and a transportation schedule to the airport, shopping, and church.

After dinner you are on your own. Don't worry about sleeping in a strange place; you will be so exhausted that the only thing you need to worry about is getting up in time to make your first class in the morning.

Allow yourself extra time this first morning. You are required to make your bed every day and to keep a clean and neat room. You will want to look your absolute best, and you will be sharing a bathroom. You will need time to decode the map to find your classroom.

Your first classroom experience will be somewhat of a shock. You will look around at the classmates you have not yet seen. There will be some wondering about how she or he ever got here—old jokes about hiring out of the telephone book, establishing the pecking order, forming cliques and alliances. Hey, just like high school, right? *Wrong*! Enjoy it while you can. The resemblance ends when the instructor walks in the door.

Your instructor has been assigned to the Training Center on the basis of past record, merit, and ability. Some assignments are temporary, some are permanent.

Whatever the case, these instructors are extremely good at what they do. They have an uncanny ability to spot those who will be successful and those who will not, within one day more or less of observing classroom performance. They know when to be your buddy and when to step down hard. Never be fooled into taking either behavior personally. It is not and cannot be personal. Your instructor has only one objective: to make you a competent flight attendant. If that is not possible, you will be dismissed no matter how much anyone likes you.

Some airlines supply pretraining study material to be learned by the beginning of training. If that is the case, you will have your first written test directly after introductions on the first morning of training. If you want to see the second morning of training, you had better be prepared.

The testing process varies slightly among airlines, but only as to the required grade number and methodology. You may have a written test daily, combinations of written and oral tests, or demonstrations of practical ability on material covered. Passing grades range from 80 percent to 95 percent according to the airline's policy. You may or may not be allowed to retake the test, again based on policy. Rest assured, you will be informed of the testing policy of *your* airline at the beginning. Expect no deviations therefrom.

Every night will be a finals cramming night. Some people will be luckier than others in ease of assimilating and understanding the subject matter. A great deal of memorization is required. Everyone is in the same boat. Learn it or sink.

You will be amazed at the closeness you will develop with your classmates. Within a week no one or nothing else matters to you except this thing: *pass*. The pressure becomes incredible, bonding you even more closely with your new best friends, with aviation, and with *your* airline. How do you survive?

It might help to know that this is exactly what flight attendant training is all about: teaching you how to survive. Those who cannot will be left behind. It is a painful process but a necessary one that most people do not understand until much later. The psychology of flight attendant training has been very carefully developed and constantly improved upon to place you under controlled pressure until you have almost reached your physical, mental, and emotional breaking point, and then to relieve that pressure with less stressful subject material until an equilibrium is reached. The intensity then begins to build again until the next plateau is reached, and so on through the process until one day a qualified flight attendant pops out the other side.

You may think that that is mean and sneaky, but it is not. It is the kindest way to prepare you for things you have never considered until now, not even in your wildest dreams. I'll tell you about them in just a bit, but for now let us return to the classroom and find out some of the things you will need to learn. If you can prepare yourself in advance, the material will not be so foreign to you and the pressure may be somewhat lessened.

Flight Attendant Curriculum

Two things determine the curriculum of your training: the Federal Aviation Regulations (FARS) and the individual requirements of your airline.

It is required by law that flight attendant training include the following areas:

- Duties and responsibilities of crewmembers
- Appropriate portions of your Flight Attendant Manual

- Appropriate portions of the FAR
- Emergency training (several specific areas)
- Authority of Pilot-in-Command
- Passenger handling
- Public address system and other methods of communication
- Physical characteristics of each aircraft on which you are to serve
- Proper use of galley and other electrical equipment and controls

For crewmembers serving in operations above 25,000 feet (jets), the following are required also:

- Respiration
- Hypoxia
- Duration of consciousness without supplemental oxygen at altitude
- Gas expansion
- Gas bubble formation
- Physical phenomena and incidence of decompression

This is actually a great deal more detailed than it looks. These are the subjects that must be covered by law. Then there are things that *your* airline needs to cover for background, and several subjects concerning company policy.

A typical five-week training program for a major airline looks something like this:

Week One: General subjects, including airline codes and terminology, company organization and structure, company rules and regulations, philosophies, FARS, schedules, airport tour, introduction to service, twenty-four-hour clock.

Week Two: Hair and grooming, customer service and passenger handling, uniform fittings, service practice in the mockups.
Week Three: Emergency training.
Week Four: More services and service practice in the mockups including cooking food in the galley. Final uniform fittings, weigh-ins and appearance checks, first aid, high-altitude physiology.
Week Five: Role playing for customer service, bidding, union contract, observation flight, domicile assignment, security training, graduation.

As for the specific subjects, you can do much to prepare now. One thing you should *not* do, in my opinion, is to pay to attend a Flight Attendant Academy that is not affiliated with an airline. TWA, for example, hires only from its own Flight Attendant Academy, but it has protections and financial assurances. I am talking about businesses that have no connection with any airline and that charge large fees without being able to guarantee you employment as a flight attendant upon completion of the course. They promise to "assist" you in securing employment, but that means only that they send huge envelopes full of résumés out to all the airlines. As a Director of Inflight, I used to get them all the time. These places have no screening process, just financial fitness checks. Most of the people who attend these schools and go on to be hired by an airline have what it takes and would be hired regardless. Those who don't have "it" won't get "it" here. If you are still convinced that you need this, then by all means go. I am just advising you that from my personal and professional point of view I can see no advantage proportionate to the cash expenditure required. However, there may be those who would disagree with me.

Preparation can make your life a little easier, but it is

not necessary for most. If you would like to have such an advantage when you get to training, study things like the airline terminology in Appendix II. Check the library for instruction books for flight attendants and airline personnel. Write to the Government Printing Office for a catalog of publications on aviation-related subjects. Some are free; others are available at a nominal charge. A friend who is already a flight attendant will be the most help of all. Ask for any old training materials he or she may have saved. No one will let you borrow her Flight Attendant Manual, but she might let you see it.

Before we go on to the really tough stuff, a few more comments on training in general. Besides your grades and comprehension, you will be studied minutely for any deficiency in personality, deportment, obedience to the rules, appearance, weight, cooperation with your classmates, attitude, language and grammar, personal habits, on-time performance, and participation. Nobody is perfect, of course, but you had better be as close to it as you can. Your instructors and the other employees of the Training Center know exactly what to look for in behavior evaluation. You must practice constant self-discipline. An unguarded moment that reveals dissatisfaction, a careless sarcastic comment will raise a red flag signaling that you might be a less than ideal employee.

Emergency Training

The primary objective of the flight attendant is the safety of the passenger. Service and comfort are secondary considerations. They are marketing tools, used to differentiate one carrier from another in the competitive world of scheduled flying. Everything you do in training—the psychological plateaus, the stress, the discipline—is structured to encourage the survival instinct. The weak are left behind. They break. They go home. They do not survive the altered environment.

This serious training is required because sometimes the unthinkable happens: Sometimes airplanes crash. If this does occur, you need to know how to best handle yourself and others. You need to be confident in your ability to deal with the situation.

The emergency week of training is the time when you really find out if you are cut out for this business. When I teach, this is where I usually give my "hearts and flowers" speech. I ask my trainees to look into their minds and hearts and ask themselves if they have the psychological makeup to discipline their own instincts and react in an emergency for the well-being of all concerned. You are told some stories and shown some things that have the potential to really scare you. The purpose of this training is to replace fear with knowledge and ability. . . .

With the closeness that develops among students sharing the training experience, it is wrenching when someone leaves. The greatest attrition rate occurs during emergency training. Some are weeded out, some choose to retire. I want you to know that it is okay for this to happen. Not everyone was made to be a flight attendant. Some people just can't. That is no reflection on them as human beings, nor does it make us better or them worse. It simply is.

Emergency training is a physical and mental exercise designed to instill confidence, retrain and refine instinct, and teach you to reason and react without even being aware of the process. It works so well that you will be amazed at a part of you that you did not know existed, the strong and commanding side of your nature that hides beneath the smooth surface, simply biding its time.

You will be drilled in the use of oxygen, the classes of fire and the use of fire extinguishers. You will open aircraft doors and windows and inflate life vests. You will go swimming with all your clothes on and wrestle with a thirty-five-person life raft. You will go down an emergency slide from the aircraft door to the ground. You will stumble around in an aircraft mock-up filled with smoke. You will learn each and every piece of emergency equipment on every airplane you fly and how and when to use it. You will leave the manners and gentility you have been practicing for the first two weeks of school at the door of the classroom and learn to become a stern commander. You will dissect accident investigations to learn from past mistakes.

You will be given facts about the safety of flight. It is true that it is more dangerous to drive to the airport than to fly on a plane. It is true that more people are injured in their homes each year than are injured in airplane crashes. It is true that at least 80 percent of all aircraft accidents are survivable. It is true that you could fly every day for over two hundred years before your statistical number comes up. It's just that no one tells you those things when the media are stirring up a circus about the accidents they cover. Flying is the safest mode of transportation yet devised, and it gets even safer with each lesson learned and each technological improvement added.

If all that is true, and I swear it is, how come you have to be subjected to this unpleasant curriculum at all? Would not a passing mention do it? No. Part of the reason flying is so safe is that the crews are trained to deal with potential problems before they result in an accident, and when something does happen you are trained to survive, command, and evacuate, thereby insuring the minimal amount of damage.

I can hear your questions now. The answers are:

1. Nobody expects you to go down with the ship.

2. The criterion for passing, besides grade and ability to perform the required drills, is whether I feel good enough about you to put my mother on your airplane.

When emergency training is complete, you are no longer a neophyte. The rest of the training, while still intense, is a snap in comparison to what you have been through. All the basics are under your belt, and what is left is polish and practice. It will take a few days to get the emergency part of things out of your head and gear your thinking back to service. Eventually, everything straightens itself out, and you become an integration of the two poles of your job.

Class Seniority

Seniority in the training center varies, depending on the airline. The most common way of determining seniority is your age: The oldest is the most senior. After fifty years, some airlines finally have concluded that people cannot do much about their age. Many airlines now determine seniority based on aggregate classroom test scores. Some airlines use a lottery system for a seniority number, and others use your social security number.

Whatever method is used, you are assigned a seniority number within your class structure. Based on your class order, you are added to the system seniority list. You also are posted in your respective domiciles in that same order.

Class seniority is used for bidding your observation flight. I was really low on the pole; we determined by age. I got to go to Moline, Illinois. I wanted to go to Los Angeles. I was really homesick by then, so I did not enjoy Moline. I almost quit. I stayed only because I didn't want everyone back home to think I'd given up; I figured I would wait until after graduation.

On the last day of training, my class got to bid on our domiciles. I wanted Los Angeles. I got Chicago. All the L.A. openings had gone in the first seven numbers. I was number 52 in a class of 55. When it got down to me, there were three Chicago openings and one Newark opening left. I took Chicago for three reasons:

1. I did not have to put all my luggage on an airplane, since I was already there.
2. My training roommates, now my best friends, were staying in Chicago.
3. I was going to quit anyway. I mean, first Moline, now Chicago? What were they trying to do to me?

5

Takeoff: Life on the Line

After the safety briefing the flight attendants proceed to their jumpseats. Typically, these fold down from the walls (bulkheads) much like the extra seats in a cab. Do not be fooled by their flimsy appearance, however. Jumpseat design and construction must conform to rigid requirements by the Federal Aviation Administration.

The seats are equipped with a shoulder harness in addition to the lap or seatbelt. Sometimes passengers ask why you have a shoulder harness and they do not. FARs require that all flight attendants use a seat with a harness, although the additional safety is only marginal. The cost of installation makes it too expensive to equip all seats on the plane with a harness.

When the plane has finished taxiing, it is positioned on the edge or threshold of the runway. The cockpit crew is cleared for takeoff, conditions permitting. A signal is given to the cabin crew to alert them that takeoff is imminent. Sometimes an announcement is made over the intercom; many passengers think the message is meant for them. Sometimes the signal is a bell or chime or a light on the annunciator panel. As a passenger, you may have heard or seen this and not realized what it meant. The signal alerts the flight crew that the plane is about to take off, unless anyone has a problem, and that everyone had better be seated.

The cockpit crew engages the brakes and brings the thrust levers slowly forward to achieve power. The brakes are released, and the aircraft begins to move down the runway, rapidly gaining enough speed to leave the ground. Good flight attendants should at this time be reviewing their emergency procedures and keeping an eye on the cabin. Bad flight attendants will be reading a newspaper or a magazine. Most flight attendants are good, especially when the Training Center is fresh in their mind. Bad habits are picked up later.

After graduation, you are required by FAR to have "Initial Operating Experience," or IOE. (Airline people abbreviate whenever possible as part of their club language.) That means that you cannot be assigned a flight as a working and required crew member until you have flown for five hours under supervision and been deemed competent. In smaller airlines, you will have your IOE with an inflight supervisor or check flight attendant. In the larger carriers, you will fly with an on-the-job trainer (OJT) approved for this function. It is usually someone who has been at it for a while. If you are lucky, the OJT is good and willing to let you work in the real world. If you are unlucky, you may draw someone who is in it for the extra money and would rather you just sat down and stayed out of the way. You can't learn that way.

I mentioned the real world. This is real life as opposed to the ideal painted in the Training Center. For instance, I was puzzled for months about how people always knew that I was new. I finally figured out that it had to do with the way I looked. My purse was the same size as when I got it—not ballooned out with junk to four times its original shape. My shoes were shined. I wore my regulation hairstyle and the approved amount of jewelry. My hat (yes, hat) was not smashed to pancake style, and I wore my gloves *and they were still white*. I remember thinking that no matter how long I flew, I always wanted to be new if being old meant looking like some of the other attendants I saw.

I do not know if I succeeded, but I always tried and have continued to do so through five airlines and twenty years, most especially when I was the boss. It's a long story how I ended up with such a checkered history. Maybe I'll tell you someday, but for now I'll give you a hint: It has to do with that merry-go-round I mentioned in Chapter 3. As you have probably guessed by now, I did not quit after graduation. I have threatened to quit at least a million times since, but I have rarely followed through with it. When I did leave a company, it was never in a moment of anger or because I had had a bad trip. It was a well-thought-out decision that was necessary to the demands of my personal life at the time. I may never really quit. Every time I left flying, I could not get back fast enough. You cannot quit what becomes a basic element in the psychology of your being. Not everyone feels this way, of course, just most of us. I am quite certain of one thing, however: I probably will threaten to quit at least a million more times before I'm through, and so will you.

This chapter is about life on the line, what it really is like to fly, the honest truth, not a recruiting film. It has been said, mostly by pilots, that flying is hours and hours of incredible boredom, punctuated by moments of stark terror. Well, okay for them, they do not have to take care of hundreds of passengers. I doubt that you will ever be bored, and in general the only terror you will ever experience will be realizing that you are not going to get to New York before Bloomingdale's closes.

Flying is like everything else in life: a sampling of experiences that are good and bad, happy and sad, and sometimes very funny. The problem is that you rarely realize what is funny until you look at it in retrospect.

The funny parts are generally awful when they are happening. One of the tricks to being a happy flight attendant is to see the humor of a situation while it is happening.

Many books have been written about people's flying experiences and in all probability will continue to be written. The public is fascinated by the "glamour" of jet travel and the mystique of flight crews. They long for behind-the-scenes stories that bring them in contact with what they perceive to be a fast track and an unorthodox lifestyle. The true paradox lies in the fact that we are just normal people who of necessity live a little differently from people who work in a bank. I say a bank because it is sort of an inside joke: If someone is complaining, we tell them to go back to the bank. When things get difficult, we say we should have stayed at the bank. I guess that is because for years the bank was the primary symbol of the rigid and stable institutional environment. One of my ex-roomies now works in a bank; I must ask her if she ever says she should have stayed on the airplane.

There is a high probability that your first trip will be the single most awful thing that has ever happened to you. Of course, three months later it will be the funniest experience of your life and you will be wondering if you have enough material yet to write a book. Hold your horses, future flight attendants; this is just the beginning.

Now comes the part where everyone who does write a book like this gets to tell their story. I bow to convention.

My airline had given me a hotel room for five days, during which time I had to complete my IOE and find a place to live. After that, I was on reserve and fair game for the crew schedulers.

In keeping with the "bunch" concept, six of us from training decided to live together. None of us had ever lived on our own before. I guess we figured there was safety in numbers.

We moved into what was then termed a "zoo" or, more appropriately for the times, a "stew zoo." It wasn't as bad as it sounds. Several enterprising apartment owners decided to fill their buildings with new flight attendants by offering certain inducements, such as larger furnished units that could accommodate several tenants and an hourly van service to the airport. Since only one of us had a car or furniture, this seemed to be the ideal solution.

So we rented a three-bedroom suburban townhouse and set about housekeeping. Funny, housekeeping was the last thing going on there. None of us could cook, and we certainly were not into dusting and polishing. We weren't too great at grocery shopping either. Once someone went out for food and came back with a case of Jell-O. I cannot eat it to this day, but I am amused when someone else orders it.

My IOE was a Seattle turnaround. That means I left Chicago in the morning, flew to Seattle, and came back the same day. The trip itself was fairly uneventful, except that during that trip I saw some experienced flight attendants display some bad habits.

I returned from Seattle undaunted, however, and by this time I had not thought about quitting for at least a week. Then I got the phone call. It was someone responsible for crew scheduling, advising me that someone had called in sick and that I was to report to the airport in two hours to cover the trip. This was it: my first flight on my own.

"Oh, boy, I'm really here, and it's finally happening. I am a flight attendant," I thought.

I was so excited that I did not even ask where I was going. If I had, I would have known why the other person was sick.

The trip sequence was something like this:

Airline Language		*English*
ORD	MKG	Chicago to Muskegon
MKG	LAN	Muskegon to Lansing
LAN	MKG	Lansing to Muskegon
MKG	ORD	Muskegon to Chicago (can't get off)
ORD	MKG	Chicago to Muskegon
MKG	FNT	Muskegon to Flint

And that was just the first day. The next two days looked just as bad.

"What? First Moline, now this! I know I signed up for Honolulu!" Welcome to the real world.

I managed to find my way to my mailbox and the check-in desk. I managed to find my airplane. That was the best it was going to get, for this trip anyway.

I boarded my aircraft and came face to face with my flying partner. We had graduated from the Training Center together, and she was on reserve as well. There seemed to be a rash of people that this trip was making sick. Anyway, we were really happy to see each other until we realized that neither of us had the slightest idea what we were doing. I know, I had just been through five weeks of training. I must have learned something, but I could not for the life of me remember what it was. My partner was similarly afflicted.

While we were staring at each other in bewilderment, a supervisor came walking down the aisle. She was there to give us a check ride. She was under the impression that this was our second trip, and she was to do a progress evaluation.

Most flight attendants do not care to see supervisors at any time and go to great lengths to avoid them, but I have to tell you that I was really glad to see this one.

She said that this type of situation was not supposed to happen, but it was too close to departure to do anything about it. Now, according to the union contract a supervisor cannot do any work defined as flight attendant duties. Within the guidelines, however, she verbally assisted us the best she could. I'm sure we must have looked pretty pitiful.

The passengers boarded, and we buttoned up and did our show and tell. So far, so good. We took off and waited for the seatbelt sign to go off. We got up. In those days, instead of inflight smocks that are much like aprons, we had a completely separate inflight dress. I changed first, then my partner changed. We found the service cart. It was the type that folded and had to be set up from scratch—no preset roll-out for us. We put everything on it we figured we'd need to do our service. We rolled it up the aisle to the first row of the coach section and asked our first passengers for their selection of beverage. The Fasten Seatbelt sign came on. The No Smoking sign came on. The supervisor was standing in the back making exaggerated motions for us to get the cart to the galley, tear it down, and put it away, *now*. We had served only one passenger each. We ran, dragging the cart behind us. We tore it down. We collected the trash. We strapped in for landing.

After we landed, I changed back into full uniform. I am talking the whole thing—hat, coat, scarf, gloves, everything. I don't know where I thought I was going, but I stationed myself at the head of the coach cabin to say good-bye to my passengers. Every single one of them asked me if it was my first trip. I wondered how they knew? I was too new to be aware that I had just participated in a disaster of the first magnitude and every flight attendant's worst nightmare: not finishing the service.

So it went for the next five legs. There was no sequence over thirty minutes in the air, but by the time I got to Flint I could set up, serve, tear down, and clean up with the best of them. I was also hungry. Neither of us had eaten or been to the restroom (except to change into that blasted inflight dress) for nine hours. There just was no time. But now all was forgotten because I was going to have my first layover.

My partner and I ran to our hotel room and changed into "civvies." We managed that rather rapidly, as you might imagine, considering all the practice we had by now in changing clothes. We left our room, only to find out that nothing is open in Flint after 9 p.m. I have often thought that trips like this were designed to make sure flight attendants stay within their weight guidelines. To this day I cannot look at a bag of peanuts or a maraschino cherry. They fall into the same category as Jell-O. You haven't lived until you have flown six legs and eight hours with nothing to eat but the cocktail garnishes.

At any rate, three days later I returned to Chicago. I listened to similar first-flight stories from my roommates, but I am absolutely positive that mine was the worst. I again vowed to quit. Soon.

As time went on, I adjusted my expectations to the reality of the situation. I realized that the only way I was going to get to Honolulu in the next twenty years was to go there on vacation. I set my sights on more attainable goals, like trying to stay out of Michigan and just doing the best I could with whatever fate and the crew desk had in store for me.

But really, Michigan wasn't so bad, especially after I got snowed-in in Cleveland, frostbitten in Des Moines, bug-bitten in Birmingham, food poisoning in New Jersey, the flu in Philadelphia, and lost on the subway in Boston. On the positive side, I also got to shop at Bloomingdales, sunbathe in Miami, see a show in Las

Vegas, eat seafood in San Francisco, and listen to jazz in New Orleans.

I have seen the wonder in the eyes of a ninety-year-old man on his first airplane trip. I have seen appreciation for a small kindness in the face of a passenger who was on her way home to bury a loved one. I have heard fear in the voices of young servicemen on their way to Seattle, the dissemination point for posting to Vietnam. I have also been screamed at, propositioned, pinched, thrown up on, and handed dirty diapers. One thing about passengers, they come in every shape, size, and temperament.

There are a lot of really great stories, some that happened to me, some that happened to my friends. Many are funny. Some are so ridiculous that if they hadn't happened to me I would never have believed them. Some of them never happened to anybody but have been around so long that they are mainstays in the industry. Some are terrifying, and some are so heroic that you wonder if you would have behaved nearly so well. Most of them have to do with passengers and something they said or did.

You need to be aware that a great many people are terrified of flying. Sometimes you know, sometimes you have to look for it. Once you understand this and learn to deal with it, you will be much better off. For the most part, a person who is afraid of flying is embarrassed to have anyone know. The outward behavior ranges from borderline catatonia, to bravado or loud obnoxious behavior, to physical manifestations such as crying, hyperventilating, or shaking uncontrollably.

The hardest to deal with, of course, are the loud-mouths, especially if their behavior becomes abusive. If being nice to them, ignoring them, or attempting to reason with them does not work—which in general it does not—your only option is to get tough. Remember,

I am not talking about passengers whose bad behavior is caused by alcohol or drugs; they are dealt with differently. The only way to handle a passenger who misbehaves to hide fear of flying is to replace the fear with an even greater and more immediate fear: being arrested. It is a federal crime to interfere with a flight crew in the performance of their duties. That fact and the threat alone should give you all the clout you need to turn this raving maniac into a pussycat. As long as you know that the person is not behaving in a personal manner toward you, you can cope more easily with the situation.

Let us examine the other side of the behavioral coin. The first scenario was the worst, obviously, because even though you successfully dealt with the situation, there was little satisfaction to you in doing so. The circumstance still exists for the person and will rise another day unless he or she gives up flying or gets professional help. In any case, it is no longer your problem.

But suppose you could help someone. Wouldn't that be great? I'll tell you a story that happened to me.

I was working as an extra flight attendant on a 727–100 charter to New Orleans. The 727 requires only three F/As, but I decided to go along to help work the meal service. Did I neglect to mention that I was Director of Inflight at the time? That is how come I "decided" to go. At any rate, we were taxiing out to the runway, and I was seated on the rear jumpseat at the center and aft of the cabin. I was minding my own business, not reading, of course, because I am a "good" flight attendant, when a woman seated about three rows forward of me turned around. She started to stare at me. I smiled. She smiled. I waved. She waved. I looked away, but when I looked back she was still staring. No runs in my stockings, no holes in my uniform. I waved again. She waved. What is this? I began to think I was in the Twilight Zone. She kept staring at me through the rest of the taxi, the takeoff, and the climb-out. By that time I was somewhat uncomfortable, to say the least. This was definitely a first, even for all my years of flying.

As soon as it was safe to get up, I went to her and asked if I might be of service. She told me that flying was agony to her, and the way she got through the flight was to watch the flight attendants for signs of panic. She figured that if they were behaving normally, things must be normal. Well, that was a new one on me, but if it made her happy, I told her, she could watch me all she wanted. I got her a drink right away and made sure she never had an empty glass. I don't think I ever smiled as much in my life as I did on that trip. I wanted that poor woman to know that everything was peachy. If I was in the galley and we hit a small bump, I popped out and waved to her. Sure enough, she was jumping up like a jack-in-the-box trying to see me. I was really her lifeline in every sense of the word. When it came time to land, I asked the person sitting next to her to move to an empty seat a few rows forward. He did not mind at all, his arm having previously been clawed during takeoff. Being an extra above the crew complement, it was not necessary for me to be positioned on a jumpseat. I sat next to the woman and talked her through the landing. She nearly collapsed with relief the second the wheels hit the runway. I needed first aid for the nail marks on my left arm, but I really felt good. Does that make sense? Yes, but only if you are a flight attendant.

6

The Service

The point at which the flight attendants get up from their jumpseats to begin cabin service generally depends on three things: the type of service offered by the airline, the number of people to be served on that flight, and the length of the leg to be flown that day. The flight attendants are briefed by the cockpit crew about what altitude or what time it is safe to be moving about the cabin. Unless otherwise necessary, flight attendants prefer to stay seated until cruising altitude has been achieved. That is not because they are lazy. It is hard on the feet, legs, and back to be up too soon because of increased stress caused by the thrust needed for takeoff and climb-out.

The airline industry is essentially a service industry. It has been service-oriented since the very beginning, when the first flight attendants (then stewards) carried picnic lunches and Thermos bottles of coffee aboard for their passengers.

In the years since, the industry has come full circle: From chefs carving prime ribs in the aisles during the 1960s, to flight attendants offering peanut-butter sandwiches during deregulation, to the chefs again, twenty-five years after their first introduction.

The Deregulation Effect

Deregulation has had an enormous effect on the airline

industry. About seventeen years ago, before deregulation, if an airline wanted to fly from Los Angeles to Chicago, it had to apply to the Civil Aeronautics Board (CAB). (The CAB no longer exists. We now have the Department of Transportation to take care of regulatory work.) Only the CAB could give an airline authority to fly that route, or any route for that matter, and the CAB set the fare for doing it.

As a consequence, maybe three carriers flew Los Angeles to Chicago. They all left within fifteen minutes of each other, and they all charged the same fare, since they had to. At times each flew only one-third full, and that is not a money-making proposition for anyone. Since the departure times were almost the same and the price was the same, the only real choice the passenger had was which of the three airlines he or she preferred. The only difference between the airlines was service. To lure the passenger, the service became more and more elaborate.

Finally, it was decided that real competition in the marketplace would be good for everyone, the airlines as well as the public. The movement toward this competitive atmosphere was called deregulation.

The deregulation of the airline industry took place in 1978. The CAB was ordered to dissolve (or, more appropriately, to ride off into the sunset, since the order was termed the "Sunset Bill"), and the marketplace opened for competition. If Imaginary Airlines wanted to fly to a certain city, it could just publish a schedule and go there. It could charge anything it wanted, marking the beginning of the "Great Fare War." New airlines sprang up everywhere, literally overnight. The fares became so unrealistically cheap that the airlines did not make enough profit to offer the type of service that once was the mainstay of the industry.

In fact, there wasn't enough money available to pay

the bills, and bankruptcy legalities were learned by airline crews in the same way that they learned about contract legalities. How long a carrier stayed in business was directly proportionate to the amount of money it could afford to lose. If a market pair had no competition, the ticket price was outrageously high; often there was no service at all, simply because it was no longer necessary to be competitive. You could fly Imaginary Airlines to your destination or you could drive. "No-frills" became the byword of the industry and the butt of comedy routines.

Then guess what happened. If a route had no competition on Saturday, three carriers were in the market by Sunday. The flying public had no idea who was flying where on any given day and no idea whether it would cost $29 or $114 to get to the place it cost $50 to fly to yesterday.

As the dust clears, we find that theory, however well-intentioned, does not necessarily translate into reality. We now have what you see today: less competition, not more. The remaining megacarrier airlines are the survivors of mergers, acquisitions, foreclosures, expansions, and streamlining, and the smaller airlines are code-sharing regionals. For every deregulation startup that has been successful, you probably can find twenty-five that were not. The Great Fare War now is still discussed only in hushed voices behind the closed doors of the boardroom, or by aviation relics like me who remember those times. A sure indication that things have come full circle is that the chefs are back.

SERVICE TODAY

There are many types of service today. They are regulated by stage or leg length and by competition in the marketplace. To understand service, you first need to know about flight time.

Flight time begins when you block out—that is, from the time the chocks are removed from under the tires and you leave the gate—to block in, when you are completely parked at the destination gate. If a published schedule says it takes 55 minutes to go from Las Vegas to Los Angeles, that includes taxi time on both ends, which is usually put at about 10 minutes. That means you have 45 minutes in the air. Now, subtract the time after takeoff until it is safe to stand up, another 3 to 5 minutes, and you have only 40 minutes to serve cocktails, soft drinks, coffee, tea, champagne, and peanuts to a full airplane, restock or tear down your cart, clean the cabin, and put everything back the way it was. At least no one has to change clothes anymore. That helps, but you do have to move some kind of fast.

Many times people think the flight attendants are mean or cranky on these flights. Not usually, just busy. If anything out of the ordinary happens, you can say good-bye to any hope of completing your service in the time allowed. This type of service is very precisely timed. If, for instance, you have an F/A just out of school, the coffeemaker is clogged, or a passenger becomes ill, it borders on the impossible to serve a full load of people and secure the cabin in time to land. Some passengers do not understand and complain loudly, making the flight attendants feel worse than they already do. If your flight line is made up of a lot of these short trips, you will surely feel as though you have run a marathon by day's end.

A good deal of time may be spent during training in introducing you to the different types of services for *your* airline. The length and intensity of this training varies with the size and route structure of the carrier. With a major airline, for instance, you may have thirty or more services to learn, ranging from continental breakfast, which is just coffee, juice, and a roll, to elaborate gourmet dinners.

You will be taught to read a catering sheet and check it against the service required and the supplies boarded. You will learn how to cook, reconstitute, set up, and garnish appetizers and entrees. You will learn the basics of wines, how to open and how to pour, what glasses to use for which wines and cocktails. In first-class service, you generally will not use the liquor miniatures we have all come to associate with the airline industry; rather you will learn to pour, mix and garnish cocktails from liter or quart bottles. You will learn what brand names equate to what kind of liquor, so that if someone asks for a blended whiskey you will know what to offer. You will learn to pour coffee from a silver service and toss a caesar salad. You will learn how to fold a linen napkin into a roll basket and how to wrap it around a bottle of champagne. Everything will be served from a silver tray or a display cart.

Back in Chapter 2, I suggested that you consider taking a course in gourmet food and wine. Now you know why. If you happened to miss that, as well as the restaurant experience I also recommended, it might be a good time to take a trip to the bookstore or library. Start with a bartending guide. Learn the brand names of liquors and liqueurs and the names of cocktails and how to make them. Keep it simple, though. You may be called upon to make a Screwdriver, Bloody Mary, Manhattan, or Martini, but the really outrageous drinks either come prebottled or you cannot serve them. Luckily, no one has yet put a blender in the galley. Some guides have diagrams or pictures of glasses with their names. You should learn the difference between a rocks glass, an old-fashioned glass, a martini glass, and a chimney glass. While you are at it, check out the wine, aperitif, and liqueur glasses, too. They all have different names and uses.

Next, get a gourmet cookbook. You need not learn how the dishes are prepared, but you do need to know what they are and how to pronounce them. Look for a book with a glossary and start there. If you do not know that "terrine of turbot" is a fancy name for fish, you have some work to do. You also need to do a quick checkup on sauces. Passengers do know the difference if you give them the hollandaise on their filet and put the béarnaise on their asparagus.

This may sound a bit intimidating, but you can learn it, you really can. After all, I learned it, and the sum total of my restaurant experience at that time was working in a hamburger stand. One of the purposes of this book is to give you a head start.

As an example of what you will be serving in first class on a domestic flight, let's look at a typical dinner menu:

Cocktail Selection: Basic offerings include vodka, gin, two choices of bourbon, two choices of scotch, rum, and a blended whiskey; also, Campari and vermouth, which may be used as a mix with some of the above or served straight. Beer and brandy may also be served, as well as sherry, other wines, or champagne. You will also have a small selection of premixed cocktails such as daiquiri, mai tai, or margarita.

Hors d'oeuvres: (May be served with champagne or second cocktail)
Goose Pâté
Breaded Scallops (hot)

Appetizer: Choice of
Shrimp Cocktail

Fresh Melon with Prosciutto
Quiche (hot)

Caesar Salad

Croissant or Whole Cracked Wheat Roll with Butter Curl

Entree: (served with wine) Choice of
Roast Rack of Veal (hot)
Chicken Cordon Bleu (hot)
Cajun Salmon (hot)

Dessert: (may be served with champagne) Choice of
Hot Fudge Sundae
Cheesecake with Fresh Blueberry Sauce
Chocolate Mousse

Varied selection of liqueurs (may be served in a snifter at room temperature or in a rocks glass over shaved ice; some are mixed with coffee and garnished with a dollop of whipped cream)

Fruit and Cheese, Swiss Chocolate, or Petit Fours (may be served with port wine)

Coffee or Tea

The above service can take from three to six hours to complete. Are you thinking that it sounds like a lot of work? Suppose you work for a carrier that flies long-haul international. You will be inflight ten to fourteen hours or more. That is long enough for your passengers to have the above-mentioned dinner, watch a movie or maybe two, go to sleep, wake up, and want breakfast—gourmet, of course:

Bloody Mary, Screwdriver, Champagne
Fruit Juice
Fresh Fruit Appetizer
Choice of: Omelette/Crepes/Eggs Benedict/Steak and Eggs (hot)
Assorted Pastries/Rolls/Butter/Preserves
Coffee or Tea

Depending on the destination, several airlines are now serving ethnic cuisine, especially Asian varieties. This development comes with its own set of complications such as learning pronunciation of the offerings, correct service procedure with specialized serving tools, and menus written in Asian languages.

Working the Galley

Where do you begin to sort this out? All service starts in the galley well before the flight ever leaves the gate. The food and supplies for a service like this come in bulk packaging. All of the chicken, for instance, will be packed in one big tin tray covered in foil. If you are really lucky, it is marked chicken. If not, you are left to figure out what it is. If it is your turn in the galley, you check the passenger menu for what you are going to serve. Then you look at the catering supply list and find out if chicken is inventoried as having been boarded, and if so, how much. You check through all of the galley compartments until you find the chicken, you unwrap it, and you count it. The same goes for all your other food supplies. Next, you check your dry supplies such as china, silverware, cocktail glasses, wine glasses, linen napkins and tablecloths, salt and pepper shakers, pot holders, passenger menus, silver service, silver trays and bowls, lace doilies, ice buckets, tongs, and so on. Following that, you check for coffee, tea, milk, soft drinks, mixers, garnishes, butter curls, flowers, dry ice,

ice cubes, and crushed ice. Oh, and one more thing: Find and count all the liquor, wine, champagne, and liqueurs and sign for them.

The flight attendant(s) working the aisle positions are responsible for the actual service, but the presentation of all this wonderful food is reserved for the galley person. Besides coordinating the cooking of the various courses (all items marked "hot" on our sample menu must be cooked in the galley ovens by the flight attendant), most of the cart setup is also left to the galley. Should you be working this position, you need to set up the carts to be full, efficient, and appealing to the eye. This includes lining them with linen cloths, having silver buckets with shaved ice, and placing fruit and flowers around the food. These things are all provided for you, but this is when you can let your creative side go wild. Everyone does it a little differently, the only limitations being your imagination and whatever materials you have at your disposal. It is really a reward to be able to see something you have created give pleasure to others.

For the most part, the person working the galley stays there for the entire trip. That is not all bad if you are working in a lower-lobe galley on a jumbo. Even though you have your work cut out for you, you are better able to concentrate without interruption since you are on another floor from where the service is being conducted. You also have enough room to organize and coordinate the service. If you are working this service from a narrow-body galley, you barely have room to turn around, most narrow-body galleys being roughly the size of a bathroom. It is harder to organize here, especially if you have a less experienced partner working the aisle who decides to be helpful while squeezing in with you—not to mention passengers who try to bypass the wait by going directly to the galley and asking for what they want. They think you are being mean if you snarl (even "good" flight attendants are occasionally driven to this measure). As in every other situation we have discussed, you do the best you can and *smile smile smile*, even if you did just spill turkey gravy all over your shoes.

Working the galley is a big responsibility. Most flight attendants who work the galley do so because they like it. Usually it works out quite well, since there are more F/As who would rather not pull kitchen duty than prefer it. Personally, I always liked it. My favorite position was the lowerlobe first-class galley of the 747. On the jumbos, this was a specific bid position that required additional training and that paid an hourly premium. When I first started flying the position, I could not even cook spaghetti. Four months later, I was a (self-styled) gourmet chef. One of the hidden rewards of being a flight attendant is being exposed to constantly diversified learning experiences.

We have discussed both ends of the service spectrum, the short liquor and beverage service and the first-class service. Quite a bit falls in between, and the airlines are constantly researching and fine-tuning their product. With the exception of flights leaving before 9 a.m., all meal services are preceded by a cocktail and beverage service. Even the early-bird trips have liquor available on request. A typical luncheon or dinner service of two-hour duration would be something like this:

Cocktail and beverage service
Entire meal served on segmented tray
Cocktail and beverage service
Second coffees

For such a service all cold food is boarded on individual trays or setups. The hot entree is boarded in individual casseroles that are already placed in the ovens. Depending on the stage length, they may be placed in the ovens frozen, cold, or hot. Your catering supply sheet gives cooking instructions. If you draw galley duty today, your job is to make sure they are cooked before you need to serve them. However, you had better double-check in case the cooking instructions are wrong. You need to count the meals. *Never* take for granted that what is supposed to be there is, in fact, there. When you count the meals, look at them. If they are frozen solid and your sheet says to hold the ovens at warming temperature, you had better think again. Hungry passengers get very cranky when their chicken is frozen.

The galley itself is a funny animal. Galleys come in all shapes and sizes and can be customized to *your* airline's specifications. Most of the major airlines have ovens in all their planes. Some nationals have ovens on only the larger aircraft, and the regionals, even if they fly some jet equipment, do not have them at all. Technically, you could have one type of aircraft flying for three types of carriers and the galley configuration would be different in all of them. Besides ovens, you have compartments for storage, and some airplanes have refrigerated compartments. On most smaller aircraft, refrigeration is accomplished by placing dry ice in a regular storage compartment. You must be sure that the ice is not directly on any foodstuffs, for it will freeze them solid. Also, never touch dry ice with your bare hands. It will burn. Use a paper towel or tongs to move it. If you are walking by an airplane galley and see smoke, chances are that a flight attendant has disposed of dry ice in the trash and it has come in contact with some liquid.

Depending on type, galleys can be changed out between segments in different ways. Most galleys are rotatable. They can be unfastened in their entirety from the aircraft floor and wheeled onto the catering truck, which is raised to the aircraft by a hydraulic jack. A completely new galley (with the exception of the ovens, which are fixed) then replaces the other. Some galleys are fixed or permanantly fastened to be aircraft, but have rotatable bins that can be taken out one by one and replaced. The third type of galley is totally fixed, and each compartment must be cleared and restocked by hand, item by item.

This third type of galley usually is found on smaller aircraft that make many stops per day, and the service generally consists of only beverages. In that case, you need to make a catering list to replenish only the items on which you have run low. You must be an inventory controller and a good housekeeper. If not, either you or the flight attendants replacing you will suffer on the next leg. If the galley is dirty or understocked, you will probably be "written up" by the outbound crew, which means that your supervisor will be looking for you. If you remember, we have already learned that this is a situation you want to encounter only under pleasant circumstances.

Special Meals

All major and some national airlines offer special meals. These may be ordered by passengers when they make their reservation. A special meal should be listed on the catering sheet and on the passenger manifest with the name of the passenger who ordered it. Special meals are for passengers who have special needs, not for just anyone who might prefer something other than what is on the menu. They include:

- Diabetic meal (also for heart disease, high blood pressure, etc.)

- Specially prepared meal to conform to religious dietary laws; for example, a kosher meal
- Bland meal for ulcer sufferer
- Vegetarian meal
- Allergy-free meal for persons with severe sensitivity to wheat, milk, eggs, peanuts, shellfish, sulfites, etc.

If a person who is allergic to a substance unknowingly consumes it, he or she could suffer mild to extreme discomfort, rash, illness, and even shock and death. You must be very careful if a passenger wants to know if a meal contains peanut extract or by-product. Don't say no if you do not know for sure. Suggest ordering a special meal for the next trip. Then, perhaps, find some fruit or a salad to serve.

Special meals are packaged differently than other meals and may have different cooking instructions. Kosher meals are to be served as is, without disturbing the seals or wrappings. The same is true for any other meals having to do with religious requirements.

Crew Meals

If you are supposed to have crew meals, check for them. Be sure there is enough for both cabin and cockpit crews. Sometimes the cockpit crew have meals scheduled and the flight attendants do not. By knowing your union contract or the policies of *your* airline, you should be able to tell if they should be on board. If you do not know about the cockpit regulations, ask. It does a great deal to promote good relations and crew concept if the cockpit crew are aware that you are taking care of them. The cockpit crew meals may be all different, but they should not all be the same. One of the pilots must consume a different meal. In the unlikely event that the food is tainted, at least one qualified pilot will be unaffected and able to fly the aircraft. Aside from meal requirements, someone, usually the senior flight attendant, should check with the cockpit regularly to see if they want anything. This does not mean that pilots think you are there to supply their personal needs. Some may, of course, but we ignore them. Rather it has to do with treating them as a part of the crew and seeing to their needs as you would those of your passengers. After all, they can't exactly go get it themselves.

If meals are left over, or if you would like a beverage, you are generally free to have what you want after the passengers are served. The only exceptions are that you may *never* remove anything from the aircraft, even if it is only a throw-away, and you may *never* consume on board or remove liquor that belongs on the airplane. They will, no kidding, fire you right now. It is just not worth it.

Accounting Requirements

Finally, there is the accounting. Liquor is sold, except in first class. Forms must be filled out showing miniatures used against money received, noting any discrepancies and the reasons for them. You may have to do this every leg, or every time the liquor kits are changed. The biggest complication here is that flight attendants are notoriously lax about what they do with the money they collect. You can hardly find a flight attendant who has not laundered liquor money with a uniform at some time in his or her career. Be assured, however, if you end up washing too much money and your accounting forms are always short, you will get the dreaded "See me" note from your supervisor.

On longer flights you may also have to account for earphone or movie money. The senior flight attendant usually does the paperwork, but it is your responsibility to keep track of what you have collected. On some international flights duty-free items are also sold, and that involves a whole other accounting process.

If you are flying to another country, several forms must be filled out by each passenger and by the senior flight attendant. On international flights the senior flight attendant is sometimes called a purser. Premium pay for this position comes along with the paperwork. Not only is the purser responsible for the service and the sales accounting, but also for the paperwork having to do with customs, immigration, and agriculture. If bond liquor is found unlocked or unaccounted for, the purser may be pulled out of bed in the middle of the night to appear before a magistrate who may just decide to impound your airplane for customs violations. Don't laugh, it's true and it has happened. I have also known captains who were threatened with jail or worse in a foreign country because flight attendants were caught with restricted items such as undeclared liquor or cigarettes, even though it was their own property. In most cases it is ignorance or stupidity on the part of the offending flight attendant, but you should be aware of the serious nature of these actions. The customs and immigration laws of other countries can be complicated for a neophyte to understand. In the final analysis, if you have any doubt at all, *ask*.

Although not having much to do with service, one or two more words on foreign travel as a crew member are in order.

Guard your passport at all times. If it is lost or stolen, notify your captain or purser immediately. Do not carry large amounts of currency, especially American dollars. Do not go exploring in areas you know nothing about, and do not go alone. If none of your crew wants to go out, arrange with the concierge at your hotel to join a group tour. Always notify a person in charge of your plans and your expected time of return. Do not tell strangers in which hotel you are staying or your outbound flight number. Never let your crew luggage leave your sight for a moment. You can have a lot of fun in a foreign layover if you follow those few simple rules.

The service is finished, all money accounted for, the paperwork complete. The galley is secured and the cabin tidied. The Fasten Seatbelt sign is illuminated, and the flight attendants prepare the passengers and aircraft for landing. All the carry-on is again stowed away, seatbacks are returned to the upright position, cigarettes extinguished, and everyone is fastened in. The flight attendants do one final physical compliance check, signal the cockpit that all is well, and position themselves in their jumpseats.

As the aircraft is externally configured for landing, flaps down, power reduced, gear lowered, altitude and position computed, passengers' thoughts return to the ground and what has brought them there. It may be a business meeting, a joyful reunion, a new job, a vacation. Whatever it is, you have lost them already, for they have once again become separate and personal unto themselves. As a flight attendant, you have given of yourself to see to their comfort and needs, and yet, before the wheels have touched concrete, you are only a nameless, faceless part of the process of going from here to there.

7

Landing: The Glamour Myth

If you do decide on a career as a flight attendant, you will alternately love every second and curse the moment that you got this hare-brained idea in the first place. I suspect that after you have been flying for a time, on about the fifth leg of the day, you will be standing in a galley covered with sticky goo from a soft drink can that took its revenge by jumping out of your hand and exploding on the floor. You will be thinking about the fact that you are running two hours late, about that businesswoman who screamed at you and threatened to write a nasty letter to the airline about the tomato juice you spilled on her white suit, and about your brand-new flying partner who has been locked in the lavatory all day being airsick. You will want more than anything for that day to end, so you can go home and soak your feet in a tub of Epsom salts.

Not a pretty picture?

"But where's the glamour?" you ask.

"What glamour?" I say. Who told you there was supposed to be glamour? I didn't. You just thought that. And why did you think that? You thought the job was glamorous because everybody outside the flight attendant field thinks the job is glamorous.

That is the glamour myth.

In the beginning, people thought flying was glamorous because almost no one did it. Truly, people most admire the unattainable dream. Early flying was associated with the brave pilots of World War I, dogfights, and the Red Baron. After that came the barnstormers, the mail routes, Amelia Earhart, and Charles Lindbergh. Heady stuff, what? History happening before your very eyes. Can you imagine how this looked to Mr. and Mrs. Joe America down on the farm? They probably saved for their whole lives to take a train trip from Omaha to Chicago.

The next really glamorous thing that happened was the advent of passenger flights. Boeing 247s, stewardesses, and China Clippers. Real people could do this. But real people generally didn't. Too expensive, too crazy. "If man were meant to fly, he would have wings!" Enter the movies. Clark Gable did it. Spencer Tracy did it. Even Rosalind Russell did it. But Myrna Loy stayed home and waited for her man. Joe and Ethel stayed in Omaha and saved for that train ride to Chicago.

The DC-3 was a revolution of technology. It carried twenty-one passengers. It had sleeper berths. It had a stewardess. It had a lav. It had movie stars. It had Presidents (Air Force One hadn't been invented yet). It took almost seventeen hours (and several stops) to go coast to coast; that is, if you didn't get snowed in anywhere or break down. If you did, it was the stewardess' responsibility to arrange overnight lodgings, meals, and/or train accommodations for her passengers. No IFR back then, no Jeppeson High Altitude Charts, no Omegas. You navigated by following highways and railroad tracks. The crew broke out portable oxygen bottles for themselves when crossing the mountains. The passengers got silly.

World War II probably did as much to promote the popularity of aviation as the development of the jet engine. Every movie star in the world was out on a bond drive and being photographed doing it. Pictures of airplanes were on the front pages of newspapers in every living room in America. Even Joe and Ethel in Omaha started to get used to the idea. After all, if Barbara Stanwyck could come popping off an airplane none the worse for wear, perhaps there was something to this flying business. Then there was the matter of the military aircraft. Soldiers became pilots. The war effort needed lots and lots of pilots. It needed lots of new technology. It got both. And what do you suppose happened to all that technology and all those pilots after the war? They went into commercial aviation, of course.

I really love the stories told by some of the old-time stewardesses. If you ask them whether their flying days of the '30s and '40s were glamorous, they probably say yes. I think what they mean is that they had fun. Yet 99 percent of them left within two years to marry. Forty or fifty years also has a tendency to smooth over the less pleasant aspects of life.

I must admit, though, that listening to their stories has a great deal of appeal for me, and many even sound glamorous. Imagine serving Carole Lombard or Eleanor Roosevelt or Douglas MacArthur. But then again, imagine seventeen hours on a DC-3.

When I was flying, there were a few times when I felt glamorous: the day I got my wings, the first time I came home in my uniform, working a publicity assignment, going to England to train on a new aircraft. Divided by the length of my career in this business, that works out to about once every five years.

Reality aside, the general public perceived the relatively fast-paced airline industry much the way they thought of Hollywood: glamorous, touchable yet unattainable, and having little to do with everyday life. As the industry grew it also became more accessible, and the next generation began to look to a career in the sky as a way out and a way up. If a young woman was attractive, she needed little else to qualify. With a bit of luck, she was off the farm and on her way to the big city without having to be financially subsidized by her family, without need of advanced education, and still able to maintain her reputation as a "nice girl." If she couldn't be a movie star, she could certainly live like one, even marry one. Hey, maybe we've hit upon something here. The glamour is not in the mechanics of the job. The glamour is in the opportunity. Is it any wonder Joe and Ethel's little girl preferred the airplane to the train?

Then something happened in the late 1960s. *The Book*. I won't mention the title, but it was written by two stewardesses under assumed names. It blew the lid off of the "nice girl" image and painted airline crews as hard-drinking, good-timing party animals with morals to match. Movies followed. More books, each more sensational than the last. Instead of deglamorizing the industry, it had the opposite effect. Flight crews were jet-setters, living like kings on a first-name basis with the rich and famous. Ask anybody, they'll tell you.

Instead of being outraged, the airline public relations kingpins decided to capitalize on the idea with advertising that was filled with double entendres and sexual innuendos such as the infamous: "Hi, I'm Bambi. Fly me." campaign. Not everyone was guilty of such practices, but the stigma was shared by all flight attendants working for all carriers and by the profession as a whole.

By the early 1970s, airlines were so large that you never flew with anyone in the same cabin crew twice, you had no idea of the identity of the pilots, whom you never saw (who cared anyway, because they were all old and married), airplanes were so big that passengers became a blurred mass of drink orders, layovers were so short that you had your choice of eating or sleeping, and on top of that you had to put up with the creeps who had read *The Book* and thought they could take you home like a copy of the inflight magazine.

That was about enough of that! Flight attendants everywhere stood up and said, "*I am a professional!*" "I will behave like a professional, and I will be treated like a professional." And it was true. By this time two very important things had happened. The first was that married women no longer had to end their career and, in fact, were granted maternity leave and the option to continue working until the legal age of retirement. The second thing was that the gender barrier was removed and men were hired for cabin positions on an equal basis with women. At last and forevermore, being a flight attendant had become a lifetime career commitment.

I do not intend this to be a historical treatise on the evolution of commercial aviation in America, but rather only a base sketch on which you are to draw. Suffice it to say that one thing led to another, as it always does, until you have what we see today: *Mega* everything: *mega*planes, *mega*speed, *mega*service, *mega*crews, and *mega*passengers. Translation: big, fast, crowded, and impersonal.

You must have heard the saying that old ideas die hard. That is it exactly. The perpetuation of a myth conceived by the masses in the days of your grandfather's youth, packaged and peddled by the airlines: "the glamour myth," a bit tarnished and worn with the years, perhaps, but alive nonetheless.

What has this to do with you? All well and good that I have explained the myth. Myth or no myth, you still want to fly. You are willing to pay for the great times with the price of a few bad ones, and you realize that in life that is generally the way of things. Good for you! You have the picture, but that still does not say why the historical attitudes and the myth should be of personal interest to you. Knowing me by now, you have probably guessed that you are going to find out.

Remember before you picked up this book. What did you think a flight attendant was? What do your parents think? Your friends?

When I teach new flight attendants we do a little exercise you may find enlightening. After all the testing and the emergency training is over, and my students have a pretty good feel for what the flight attendant business is all about, I ask them to give me words descriptive of what they previously thought about people who do this job, or what they have heard from others. I write the words on one side of the blackboard:

smart airhead kind shallow amoral nice
mean wife loose glamorous pushy daughter
pretty

Then I pair off the students and have them and write down the qualities they see in their partner. When they have finished, we read them aloud and I write them on the other side of the board:

intelligent pretty handsome caring good-hearted leader neat persistent meticulous friend

Let's analyze what we have. On the one hand, we find that people's perceptions of a flight attendant have to do with:

1. The glamour myth of bygone days, as in *pretty*, *nice*, *glamorous*.
2. Flight attendants perceived within their own personal sphere of recognition, such as *wife*, *daughter*.

3. Pleasant or unpleasant personal experience with a flight attendant, usually the most recent, as *mean*, *kind*.
4. That other myth perpetuated by *The Book*: *amoral*, *airhead*, *shallow*, *loose*.

Perhaps you also noticed that even after almost twenty years the adjectives are generally descriptive of women. Men who decide on a career as a flight attendant still have a certain amount of historical prejudice to overcome. The only advice I can give you is that you *can* have an exciting and rewarding career in this field if you choose to do so. Besides, plenty of passengers still feel uncomfortable when they hear a soprano voice from the cockpit announce, "This is your Captain."

The other side of the coin looks like this. Trainees who have been through an intense period of time together, sharing a common bond, express their impressions with superlatives that are more in tune with reality. You will notice that, except for *handsome* and *pretty*, gender-specific adjectives are not used unless they encompass both sexes, and that the qualities described are all affirmative in connotation. Taken as a whole, the descriptions boil down to one theme: "special." If the interviewer and the trainer have done their jobs, that is exactly what you will find: a room full of exceptionally special human beings.

Here I am telling you what great people you are, and you know it's true or I would not say it, so what is the problem? The problem is *them*. You remember *them*. They are the passengers we have to serve and please every day. They are the ones who came up with the first set of words, not I. They still believe in the myth. You are not a myth; you are a human being. How can the two be reconciled? Wait, there is more.

Two areas of perceptions and expectations remain to be examined. The first has to do with the attitude of the company toward the flight attendant. The second has to do with perception of self. The second is inexorably connected to the first, although the reverse is not necessarily true.

Airlines demand certain behaviors from their flight attendants, the first of which is loyalty. This usually is achieved in the training process by inspiring a gratitude response in the trainee. You are constantly told that you are lucky to be here, that 5,000 people are standing in line to take your place if you do not "measure up"; that the company is your mentor, it is the best, you are the best, you should be proud, our flight attendants are the front line of defense to insure that we stay the best, etc. Loyalty in an employee is an admirable quality; all employers want it. Why is this case different? It is different because you are going to be asked to do something that is foreign to human instinct, and you will be asked to do it out of loyalty to the company.

The foundations for the type of behavior that will be asked of you have their roots in your basic personality. In Chapter 1, you took a quiz relating to inherent qualities you need to be a successful flight attendant. These basically have to do with a sunny disposition, liking people, being able to deal with stress, following the rules, having respect for authority, and so on. If you have these qualities, the next is somewhat easier. If you do not, you will not survive long in this field.

To the point: You will be asked and expected to perform in a genuine-false manner. While seemingly contradictory in effect, the meaning is clear. You are expected always to sublimate your personal feelings in favor of the expectations of the passengers who purchase the myth with the price of an airline ticket. They want the smile because they have paid for it, and like all myths, they want it to be genuine and feel cheated if it is not.

At first, the smiles are as easy as they are real. As the demands of service, the time constraints, large passenger loads, and unreasonable complaints take their toll on your enthusiasm, the caring, empathy, and happiness of your nature begin to take a back seat to the physical task at hand. You are puzzled because you love this job, it is the best job in the world, you are working for the best company in the world, so why don't you feel better about the whole thing?

To please your company and your passengers, you try to get "up" and you try to stay there while you are "on." Stage acting is not sufficient; it must come from inside. This may not sound difficult, but believe me, it is probably the hardest part of the job: the confusion of feeling that you still care about people yet being afraid that all the acting has made you stop caring. A great deal of anger is associated with this feeling, yet you have no freedom to express it. No display of displeasure is ever allowed. There are some who after a time begin to lose their personal identity to the myth or become unsure of their own true emotions. Some burn out, some become jaded; most find a way to handle it.

Understand that a smile may not be all that was purchased. Some passengers have very personal ideas about the myth and what they expect to encounter. They want to see whatever they think a flight attendant is. Go back to the words earlier in the chapter. They may expect any one or a combination of those personality or appearance traits, and they are disappointed when not rewarded. I have seen passengers in a state of shock because they have seen a flight attendant eat or go into the lav. They simply did not expect you to function as a human being. A flight attendant is still a myth to a large percentage of the population, and they want to participate in the realization of that myth as part of the flying experience. The company does its best to see that they get what they want and, in general, is more or less successful even without intense supervision or overt threat and heavy-handedness. The company simply tells you what it expects of you, and because you are the kind of person you are, you comply in an effort to please. Your company may treat you well, pay you handsomely, and deal with you fairly, all to their credit. However, safety notwithstanding, in actuality your position is a "marketing tool," and your primary objective is to sell the company. If it takes a chip out of your heart or puts a little rip in the fabric of your individual self, well, whoever said it was easy?

What of flight attendants as persons? How do they learn to cope, and how do they perceive themselves? The answer thereto is the key to success, survival, and happiness.

First and foremost, as a flight attendant you must have self-respect. Although at times you may feel for all the world like the mindless grinning drudge some say you portray, *you* know what your job is. *You* know how hard you worked to learn the skills that may one day be needed to save someone's life. *You* know you can and will do whatever is necessary to command order from chaos should that be needed. *You* know you really can make people feel better or brighten their day. All it takes is a genuine need and you will be there with a genuine response, one that comes from the heart and not from the manual.

You are so many wonderful and admirable things, my dear friend, and you must never forget them. If you should forget, you will be lost to the ranks of the unfeeling. You must be proud of what you are. Carry that pride in your heart right next to respect, and save a little room for humor and wonder. They are all miracle medicines that have the ability to return that which time steals. Try to remember the excitement of the applications and the interviews, waiting for the mail carrier, and the day you looked back down that long jetway and saw Mom crying, Dad with his arm around her, the mixed tears of parting and joy that were wetting your own eyes. Feel again the closeness and sharing with your classmates during training, and the incredible sense of achievement on graduation day when you wore your very own wings for the first time. Think for a moment about all who have gone before you, those brave and visionary pioneers who gave everything they had, sometimes even their lives, to build one of the greatest industries in the world today. Therein is your legacy, therein your greatness. The contribution you make today, no matter how small you or anyone else may think, is a page in tomorrow's history, whether your name appears there or not. Keep these thoughts close inside of you, and never let anyone take them away. Only then will you know for sure why being a flight attendant really is the best job in the world.

Epilogue

Ladies and gentlemen, I would like to be the first to welcome you to your destination. It will take the captain a few moments to taxi the aircraft to the gate. Please remain seated until the Fasten Seatbelt light has been turned off.

After we reach the gate, please check around your seat and in the overhead compartments for any personal items you may have brought on board the plane.

On behalf of Imaginary Airlines and your flight crew, I wish to thank you for flying with us today on your special charter flight to the future. It has been our pleasure to serve you, and we sincerely hope that we will see you again soon.

Thank you, and have a pleasant day, wherever your plans may take you.

Appendix I
Airline Hiring Requirements and Airline Addresses

The information provided in this section is for a random group of airlines. It is included as an example of the differences between airline companies in the areas of job requirements, training, benefits, and so on. To obtain information about airlines not listed in this section, either contact the specific airline directly or visit the library to conduct some research.

American Airlines

American Airlines is one of the nation's largest airlines. First organized during the late 1920s, American has worked its way to the top of the airline industry.

American Airlines employs more than 37,000 workers, with about 17,000 of them being flight attendants. It runs major hubs at Dallas/Fort Worth and at Chicago. It also had secondary hubs in Nashville and in Raleigh/Durham.

Company requirements for flight attendants include the following:

Age:	20 minimum
Height:	Minimum 5′1½″, Maximum 6′
Weight:	Must be in proportion to height
Vision:	Correctable to 20/50
Education:	Requires high school diploma or equivalent. Prefers 2 to 4 years' college.
Language:	Preference given to applicants fluent

	in Japanese, Swedish, Spanish, French, German.
Employment History:	Prefers 2 years of public contact work.

Training for American Airlines flight attendants is completed in Dallas, and the initial program lasts 5½ weeks. Trainees are not paid by the company while they complete their training. The company does, however, provide free transportation to the training facility, and trainees receive room and board at no cost.

Domicile locations include the following:

Chicago
Dallas/Fort Worth
Los Angeles
Miami
Nashville
New York
Raleigh-Durham
San Francisco
San Juan
Washington, DC

Uniforms for graduates of American Airlines' flight attendant training are paid for by the employee. The company offers a payroll deduction installment plan to cover the cost of uniforms.

Membership in the Association of Professional Flight Attendants is mandatory for American Airlines flight attendants.

Benefits for flight attendants include life, medical, and dental insurance, which is paid for by the company.

American Airlines does not accept résumés. To apply for a job with American you should write for an application form. When you've completed the form, send it, along with a self-addressed, stamped envelope and a $20 nonrefundable application processing fee, to:

American Airlines Inc.
Flight Service Recruitment
PO Box 619410MD 4125
DFW Airport, TX 75261-9410

After you submit your application, it remains on active status for one year. Applicants selected for an interview will be transported at no cost to an interview city. Two interviews are required, and both are in a group format.

United Airlines

United Airlines was created in the early 1930s, and the company has grown steadily throughout the years to become one of the world's largest airline companies. United Airlines is a subsidiary of Allegis Inc. (formerly UAL Inc.), and the company employs about 44,000 workers.

Company requirements for flight attendants include the following:

Age:	19 minimum
Height:	Minimum 5′2″, Maximum 6′0″
Weight:	Must be in proportion to height
Vision:	Correctable to 20/30
Education:	Requires high school diploma
Languages:	Preference given to applicants fluent in Asian or European languages
Employment History:	Prefers applicants who have worked in demanding positions and who have had considerable public contact.

Training for United flight attendants is offered in Elk Grove Township, IL (near Chicago). Training lasts six to seven weeks, and the company pays for trainees' room and board. Flight attendant trainees are not paid during the training process.

Domicile locations include the following:

Chicago	Denver
Cleveland	Honolulu

Los Angeles	San Francisco
Newark	Seattle
New York	Washington, DC

Uniforms. New graduates must purchase their own uniforms, but United offers a payroll deduction plan to manage the charges. The company does assist with moving expenses to a flight attendant's initial assignment by providing seven days' hotel expense and a space-available poundage allowance to a maximum of 500 pounds.

Benefits for flight attendants include life, medical, and dental insurance, which is paid for by the company.

United Airlines flight attendants are affiliated with the Association of Flight Attendants (AFA).

If you are interested in applying for a flight attendant position at United Airlines, write for an application form:

United Airlines—EXOEL
Flight Attendant Employment
PO Box 66100
Chicago, IL 60666

The company charges a $15 application processing fee, which you should return with a completed application. After you submit your application, it will remain on file for 12 months.

Transportation to an interview city will be arranged by the company for applicants selected to complete the interview process. Two interviews are required. The first interview is in a group format. The second interview may be in either a group or private format.

Southwest Airlines

Southwest Airlines provides high-frequency air service

to more than thirty-four cities, primarily in the southwestern, midwestern, and western regions of the United States. Southwest focuses on short-flight markets. The company employs about 11,500 workers.

The company provides service between Dallas, Houston, San Antonio, the Rio Grande Valley, Austin, El Paso, Corpus Christi, Lubbock, Midland/Odessa, Amarillo, and Texas City in Texas. Southwest also flies to Tulsa and Oklahoma City, OK; Albuquerque, NM; New Orleans, LA; Little Rock, AR; Kansas City and St. Louis, MO; Phoenix, AZ; Las Vegas, NV; and San Francisco and Los Angeles, CA.

Company requirements for flight attendants include the following:

Age:	20 minimum
Height:	Minimum 5′2″, Maximum 6′4″
Weight:	Must be in proportion to height
Vision:	Correctable to 20/50
Education:	High school diploma preferred, but GED acceptable. Two years of college preferred.
Employment History:	Two years' public contact work experience desired.

Training for Southwest Airlines flight attendants is five weeks long and offered in Dallas, TX. The company furnishes no-cost transportation to the training facility, and housing is company-paid for trainees from outside the Dallas/Fort Worth area. Training is provided at no charge to the employee. Employees are not paid during the training process.

Domicile locations include the following:

Dallas	Houston
Phoenix	

Uniforms. Employees pay for their own uniforms, and payroll deduction is available for this purpose. Special "Funfare" uniforms are provided to the flight attendant at no cost.

Benefits for flight attendants include life, medical, and dental insurance, which is paid for by the company.

Southwest Airlines does not accept résumés. To apply for a flight attendant position, you must write for an application. Send a self-addressed, stamped envelope to:

Southwest Airlines
PO Box 366
Love Field
Dallas, TX 75235-1625

Completed applications should be returned with an application fee of $10.

Your application will remain active for six months. Applicants selected for interviews will be provided with transportation to an interview city if the applicant lives on a Southwest route. The hiring process requires two interviews. The first is a group interview; the second is private.

Alaska Airlines

Alaska Airlines provides air transportation to thirty-four airports in five states: Alaska, Washington, Oregon, California, and Arizona. The airline also services four cities in Mexico and three cities in Russia. Alaska Airlines is a subsidiary of Alaska Air Group Inc.

Company requirements for flight attendants include the following:

Age:	21 minimum
Height:	Minimum 5′2″

Weight:	Must be in proportion to height
Vision:	Correctable to 20/20
Education:	High school degree required. Two years college preferred.
Languages:	Preference given to applicants fluent in Spanish.
Residence:	Must establish residence within the Alaska Airlines route system (Alaska or West Coast)
Employment History:	Requires at least two years' public contact experience.

Training is conducted in Seattle, Washington, and lasts five weeks. All trainees receive a per-diem allowance, and if the trainee is from out of town, Alaska provides housing.

The company will provide space-available air freight (on line only) to assist a graduate with moving expenses to an initial assignment.

Domicile locations include the following:

Seattle
Long Beach, CA

Uniforms are employee-paid. The cost of the uniforms may be payroll deducted on an installment plan.

Benefits include life, medical, and dental insurance, which is paid for by the company, as well as a 401K retirement plan.

Alaska's flight attendants are required to join the Association of Flight Attendants (AFA).

Alaska Airlines does accept résumés, but a completed application form also is required. No processing fee is charged. To obtain an application form, send a stamped, self-addressed envelope to the following address:

Employment Department
Alaska Airlines Inc.
PO Box 68900
Seattle, WA 98168

Your application will remain active for one year. If you are selected for an interview, you can receive free transportation to an interview city if you live on an Alaska Air route. Three interviews are required during the hiring process. The first interview is in a group format. The second and the third interviews are private.

Midway Airlines Inc.

Midway Airlines provides both commercial transportation for passengers and nonscheduled passenger charter services. The airline's commercial operations include serving 54 cities in 21 states, the District of Columbia, and the Bahamas, Charter services include nonscheduled passenger flights among several cities in the continental United States and from the United States to Canada.

Midway Airlines employs about 6,000 workers, and the company maintains facilities at Midway Airport in Chicago, Illinois.

Company requirements for flight attendants include the following:

Age: 21 minimum
Height: Minimum 5′2″
Weight: Must be in proportion to height
Vision: Correctable to 20/20
Education: High school diploma or equivalent required.
College preferred.

Training is provided in Chicago and lasts four weeks. The company provides transportation to the training facility and also provides housing. Trainees receive minimum wage while completing the program.

Domicile locations include the following:

Chicago (Midway Airport)
Philadelphia, PA

Uniforms. Flight attendants must cover the cost of their initial uniform. Payroll deduction is available to cover this cost.

Benefits include life, medical, and dental insurance, which is paid for by the company. Flight attendants also participate in a 401K retirement plan.

Midway Airlines does accept résumés but also requires a completed application. When you request an application, you should enclose a self-addressed stamped, envelope.

Completed applications, along with a $10 processing fee, should be returned to the following address:

Midway Airlines
Flight Attendant Recruitment
5959 South Cicero Avenue
Chicago, IL 60638

Applications will remain on file with the company for twelve months. If you are selected for an interview, you will receive free transportation to the interview city. The hiring process requires two interviews. The first is a group interview; the last is private.

Henson Aviation Inc.

Henson Aviation is a commuter airline that is a subsidiary of USAir Group Inc. USAir provides reservations and ground support services to Henson in return for service fees. Henson Aviation operates under the name "USAir Express."

Company requirements include the following:

Age:	21 minimum
Height:	Minimum 5′0″, Maximum 6′0″
Weight:	Must be in proportion to height
Vision:	Requirement not available
Education:	High school diploma or equivalent. Some college preferred.
Employment History:	Customer-service work preferred.

Training is conducted in Salisbury, Maryland, at Henson Aviation's corporate offices. Classes consist of three weeks' intensive training. The company provides transportation to the training facility and also provides housing throughout the training period. Trainees receive a salary, beginning on the first day of training.

Domicile locations include the following:

Florence, SC
Salisbury, MD
Norfolk, VA
Jacksonville, FL
New Bern, NC

Uniform costs are split 50–50 between the flight attendant and the company for the first two uniforms. The third set is paid for by the company. Payment for the initial uniforms may be arranged through a payroll deduction plan.

Benefits include life, medical, and dental insurance, which is paid for by the company. Flight attendants also may participate in a 401K retirement plan or a Defined Benefit pension plan.

Henson does accept résumés, but you should also submit an application for employment. Send your request for an application and a self-addressed, stamped envelope to the following address:

Henson Aviation, Corporate Offices
Salisbury, MD 21801
Attn: Personnel-Flight Attendant Recruitment

Completed applications remain active for six months. If you are chosen for an interview, your transportation to an interview location will be paid by the company. Two interviews are required; both are private.

SkyWest Airlines

SkyWest Airlines is a Utah-based regional air carrier. It provides both passenger and air freight service to 42 destinations in eight Western states. SkyWest Airlines is a subsidiary of SkyWest Inc.

Company requirements for flight attendants include the following:

Age:	21 minimum
Height:	Minimum 5′0″, Maximum 5′7″
Weight:	Must be in proportion to height
Vision:	Correctable to 20/20
Education:	High school diploma or equivalent required. Two years college preferred.
Employment History:	Public contact work preferred.

Training is provided in Palm Springs, California, and is two weeks in length. The company provides transportation to the training facility (on line only), but there is approximately a $20 per day charge for lodging. Trainees receive a stipend throughout the training period.

Domicile locations include the following:

Palm Springs, CA
Salt Lake City, UT

Uniform costs are split 50–50 between the company and the employee. A payroll deduction plan is available to assist with the cost.

Employee benefits include life, medical, and dental insurance, which is paid for by the company, as well as participation in a 401K retirement plan.

SkyWest does accept résumés but also requires a completed application form. When you request an application you should include a self-addressed, stamped envelope.

Completed applications and a $15 processing fee should be submitted to the following address:

SkyWest Airlines Inc.
444 South River Road.
St. George, UT 84770
Attn: Personnel—Flight Attendant Recruitment

Applications are kept on file for six months. If you are selected for an interview, your transportation to the interview city will *not* be paid by the company. Two interviews are required for hire. The first is a group interview. It is followed by a private interview.

American Eagle (Simmons)

American Eagle is a subsidiary of AMR Corp., which is the parent company of American Airlines. American Eagle comprises six individual airline operations, including Executive Airlines, Nashville Eagle, Simmons Airlines, Wings West, and Metroflight. American Eagle operators provide transportation to 173 cities in the continental United States, the Bahamas, and the Caribbean.

Simmons Airlines provides services to six states in the Great Lakes Region.

Simmons' **company requirements** for flight attendants include the following:

Age:	20 minimum
Height:	Minimum 5′0″, Maximum 5′10″
Weight:	Must be in proportion to height
Vision:	Correctable to 20/20
Education:	High school graduate or GED. Some college preferred.
Employment History:	Customer-service work preferred.

Simmons **training** is conducted in Chicago and lasts for two weeks. Transportation to the training site is provided by the company. In addition, the company covers housing costs for trainees from outside the Chicago area. Trainees receive a stipend throughout the training period.

Domicile locations include the following:

Chicago, IL
Marquette, MI
Flint, MI

Uniform costs are split 50–50 between the company and the flight attendant. A payroll deduction plan assists flight attendants with the payments.

Benefits include life, medical, and dental insurance, which is paid for by the company.

American Eagle (Simmons) does accept résumés. In addition to your résumé, you should complete an application form. Send your application form request, along with a self-addressed, stamped envelope, to the following address:

American Eagle
Flight Attendant Recruitment
PO Box 224505
Dallas, TX 75222-4505

Your completed application form will remain on file for six months. If you are selected for an interview, the company will arrange transportation to an interview city. The hiring process requires two interviews. The initial interview is in a group format; the final interview is private.

MAJOR & NATIONAL AIR CARRIERS IN THE UNITED STATES & CANADA

Air Canada
PO Box 14000
Air Canada Center
St. Laurent, PQ
Canada H4Y 1H4

Air Wisconsin Inc.
(subsidiary of UAL Corp.)
203 Challenger Drive
Appleton, WI 54915-9120

Alaska Airlines Inc.
(subsidiary of Alaska Air Group)
Box 68900
Seattle, WA 98168

Aloha Airlines Inc.
(subsidiary of Aloha Airgroup Inc.)
PO Box 30028
Honolulu, HI 96820

American Airlines Inc.
(subsidiary of AMR Corp.)
Box 619616
DFW Airport, TX 75261-9616

American Trans Air Inc.
(subsidiary of Amtran Inc.)
Box 51609
Indianapolis International Airport
Indianapolis, IN 46251-0609

America West Airlines Inc.
4000 East Sky Harbor Boulevard
Phoenix, AZ 85034

Canadian Airlines International Ltd.
(subsidiary of PWA Corp.)
Suite 2800
700 2nd Street SW
Calgary, AB
Canada T2P 2W2

Continental Airlines
Suite 1501
2929 Allen Parkway
Houston, TX 77019

Delta Air Lines, Inc.
Hartsfield-Atlanta Intl. Airport
Atlanta, GA 30320

Hawaiian Airlines Inc.
(subsidiary of HAL Corp.)
PO Box 30008
Honolulu, HI 96820

Horizon Air Industries Inc.
(subsidiary of Alaska Air Group)
PO Box 48309
19521 Pacific Highway S.
Seattle, WA 98188

Markair Inc.
(subsidiary of Alaska International Industries)
PO Box 196769
4100 International Airport Road
Anchorage, AK 99519-6769

Midwest Express Airlines Inc.
(subsidiary of KC Aviation Inc-Appleton)
4915 South Howell Avenue
Milwaukee, WI 53207

Northwest Airlines Inc.
Minneapolis-St. Paul International Airport
St. Paul, MN 55111

Northwest Territorial Airways Ltd.
(affiliate—Air Canada)
PO Service 9000
Yellowknife International Airport
Yellowknife, NT
Canada X1A 2R3

Southwest Airlines Co.
Box 36611, Love Field
Dallas, TX 75235

Tower Air Inc.
Hangar 8
JFK Intl. Airport
Jamaica, NY 11430

Trans World Airlines Inc.
100 South Bedford Road
Mt. Kisco, NY 10549

United Airlines
(subsidiary of UAL Corp.)
Box 66100
Chicago, IL 60666

USAir
(subsidiary of USAir Group Inc.)
2345 Crystal Drive
Crystal Park 4
Arlington, VA 22227

USAir Shuttle
(Shuttle Inc.)
75–20 Astoria Boulevard
Jackson Heights, NY 11370

For information about international major carriers or any regional carriers, consult the latest National Aviation Directory, available at most libraries.

Appendix II Glossary of Airline Terminology and Abbreviations

A/C	Aircraft.
AD	Airworthiness Directive, issued by FAA, having to do with aircraft maintenance.
Aft	Toward the tail section of the aircraft.
Ailerons	Part of the aircraft used to aid turning or banking.
Airfoil	Part of the aircraft used to support lift, such as the wings or stabilizers.
Airspeed	Speed of the aircraft in relation to the air through which it is passing. Airspeed is usually read in knots.
Airstair	Stairs that are part of the aircraft. May be used for boarding or deplaning.
Alternate	Term used in flight planning to indicate a second airport at which the flight will land if unable to land at the scheduled airport.
ATA	Actual time of arrival.
ATC	Air Traffic Control.
ATD	Actual time of departure.
ATO	Airline ticket office.
Base	City from which crew members are

	assigned. Crews usually live in this city. If you do not, you are a "commuter." Your base station may also be called a "domicile."
Bid	Request to fly a schedule in order of preference. Bids are awarded on a seniority basis.
Blueroom	Old-fashioned term for aircraft lavatory. Usually it is simply called "lav," although sometimes passengers ask for the "head," confusing the airplane with a boat.
Board	Get on the aircraft.
Boonies	Remote gate, boarding point, or aircraft parking place well away from the terminal gates. Passengers and crew must be bussed to the aircraft.
Bulkhead	Any dividing wall on the interior of the aircraft.
Cabin	Section of the aircraft occupied by passengers.
CAT	Clear air turbulence, usually unexpected.
Checklist	List of items that must be completed before moving on to the next phase of flight.
Check ride	Flight on which personnel are observed by company supervisory personnel. When the FAA does a check ride, they call it an "enroute."
Cockpit	Section of the aircraft that houses the pilots; it is separated from the cabin by a bulkhead and a door.
Comail	Intransit company mail.
Comat	Intransit company materials.

Commuter	Airline crew member who lives somewhere other than at the base. Commuters use airline passes to travel to their base when they have a trip assignment.
Cycle	One takeoff and landing. This term generally is used to time required maintenance inspections.
Deadhead	Flight used to position a crew to pick up a flight or to return to base after a flight. Crew members may or may not be in uniform but sit in the cabin and ride as passengers. They are not part of the working crew.
Decompression	Loss of pressurization.
Delay	Running behind schedule.
Demo	Demonstration. Same as Safety Briefing or Show and Tell.
Deplane	Leave the aircraft.
Ditch	Emergency landing on water.
Domicile	See Base.
DOT	Department of Transportation.
ETA	Estimated time of arrival.
ETD	Estimated time of departure.
ETE	Estimated time enroute.
Empennage	Entire tail section of the aircraft.
Extra	Flight attendant assigned to a flight above the normal crew complement. This is usually done to facilitate the service.
F	Ticket designation for first-class passenger.
FAA	Federal Aviation Administration.
F/A	Flight attendant.
FAR	Federal Aviation Regulation.
Ferry	Flight to position an aircraft. This

	flight has no revenue passengers on board, but may have crew members or other company personnel.
Flight level	Altitude at which an aircraft is flying, designated numerically. For instance, Flight Level 250 indicates 25,000 ft. Flight Level 310 (pronounced three-one-zero) indicates an altitude of 31,000 ft.
Flight plan	Detailed outline of the proposed route of flight; filed by the dispatcher with air route traffic control center before departure.
Forward	Toward the front of the aircraft.
Fuselage	Body of the aircraft to which the wings, landing gear, and tail are attached. If anyone tells you the aircraft needs a fuselage change, they are pulling your leg.
Furlough	Layoff.
Galley	Aircraft kitchen. Also called a buffet.
G.O.	General offices or airline executive offices.
Ground speed	True airspeed, plus tail wind or minus head wind, at which aircraft is traveling over the ground.
Head wind	Wind blowing in the opposite direction from which the aircraft is flying. The prevailing winds usually blow west to east.
Heavy	ATC term for jumbo aircraft: 747, DC-10, L-1011.
Holding time	Unscheduled time spent on the ground with passengers on the aircraft.
Holding pattern	Also called a stack-up. Flight altitude

	and coordinates assigned by ATC for an aircraft waiting to land at a congested airport.
IAS	Indicated air speed.
IATA	International Air Transport Association.
ICAO	International Civil Aviation Organization.
IFR	Instrument flight rules.
ILS	Instrument landing system.
Inboard	Position closest to the fuselage.
Inbound	Aircraft or crew arriving at station.
INFO	Information.
INOP	Inoperative.
Jetway	Telescoping covered walkways attached to the terminal, positioned at an aircraft door for boarding and deplaning.
Knot	Unit of speed equaling one nautical mile per hour. One knot is 1.15 statute miles.
Landing	Act of terminating flight and bringing the aircraft to rest on the ground.
Landing gear	Understructure including the wheels on which the aircraft rests. The gear is retracted during flight.
Layover	See RON.
Layover station	Place where aircraft or crew rest to await another flight; can be for a few hours or overnight.
Leading edge	Forward part of any airfoil.
Leg	Segment of a flight.
LOA	Leave of absence.
Log	Flight-by-flight record of the operations of an airplane, engine, or crew,

	listing flight time, areas of operation, and other pertinent information.
Mach	Speed of sound. Aircraft speed is sometimes expressed as a percentage of the speed of sound. Mach .78 is 78 percent of the speed of sound.
Mini	Miniature, small bottle holding about one ounce of liquor.
Missed	Missed approach. Aircraft that is lined up and prepared to land but instead goes around.
MX	Mechanical problem.
MX FRY	Maintenance ferry. Positions an aircraft with a maintenance problem to a place equipped to fix it. No passengers are carried on these flights, and usually, depending on the problem, neither are flight attendants.
N/A	Not applicable, not authorized, or not available.
Non-rev	Non-revenue; person not paying for a flight, usually relating to an airline employee flying on a pass.
Ops	Operations.
Ops Specs	Operations specifications. Document signed by airline and FAA designating the parameters under which the airline will operate.
Outboard	Position farthest from the center of the aircraft.
Outbound	Aircraft or crew leaving station.
PA	a) Passenger address system. b) Announcement. c) Passenger agent.

PAX	Passengers.
Penalty box	Holding area on the airfield. Airplanes go to the penalty box to wait for a gate.
Per diem	Money paid to crew members at a set rate to reimburse them for expenses while on a trip.
PIC	Pilot in Command, usually the captain.
PIREP	Pilot report.
Pit	Baggage and/or cargo compartment underneath the passenger compartment of an aircraft.
Pressurization	Process of pumping large quantities of air into an airtight fuselage, similar to blowing up a balloon. The process keeps the inside condition of the cabin as close as possible to that on the ground. It is controlled from the cockpit.
Prop wash	Wind created by whirling motion of propellers. Sending you for a bucket of prop wash is like going in for a fuselage change.
Ramp	(a) Concrete or asphalt paving on the field side of the terminal where the aircraft parks. (b) Portable stairs rolled up to the aircraft for boarding or deplaning.
Revenue	Anyone paying for a trip.
RON	Remain over night. Same as a layover.
Rudder	Located on the tail, at the trailing edge of the vertical stabilizer, it controls the forward direction of the aircraft.

Runway	Concrete strip used for takeoffs and landings. Amber lights border the runway.
SIC	Second in Command, usually the co-pilot or first officer.
Sim	Simulator. Machine built like a part of an aircraft to simulate flight or a programmed set of circumstances, used in training flight crews.
STOL	Short takeoff and landing.
T/O	Takeoff.
Tail wind	Wind blowing in direction the aircraft is traveling. Opposite of head wind.
Taxi	To operate an aircraft on the ground under its own power incidental to takeoff or landing.
Taxiway	Concrete or asphalt ribbons over which an aircraft taxis to or from the runway. Taxiways are bordered with blue lights.
Thru	Flight or passenger originating in one city, going to another, with a scheduled stop along the way.
Turbulence	Bumpy air attributed to storm systems, mountain wave activity, heat, or wind. Usually predictable.
Turn	a) Turnaround; trip that departs and returns to the same city the same day. b) Time at the gate between arrival and departure.
UM	Unaccompanied minor. Child under twelve flying alone.
VFR	Visual flight rules.

Wake turbulence	Unstable or disturbed air caused by "heavy" aircraft engine blast.
WX	Weather
Y	Ticket designation for coach-class passenger.

Index